5:2 Fast Diet Recipe Book

Meals for One:

Amazing Single-Serving 5:2 Fast Diet Recipes to Lose More Weight with Intermittent Fasting

Diana Clayton

TABLE OF CONTENTS

Meals Around 100 Calories

DINNER Around 100 Calories 40

Meals Around 200 Calories

BREAKFAST Around 200 Calories 54

Meals Around 300 Calories

Introduction

So, you hopped on the scale and quickly hopped off again, reset it and tried again (yes, we all do that!), but alas, it's true – you are gaining a few pounds. But instead of wallowing in misery while munching that last piece of chocolate cake, you decide to do something about it. In all your proactive glory, you rev up the computer and fall safely into the arms of google, your trusty friend who has never let you down. But – BETRAYAL! – The cyber world is all abuzz with detoxing and liquid diets and you quickly feel your heart sink into your tummy. Because let's be honest, who has the willpower to endure a 3 day liquid fast where nothing passes your lips but water and the odd fruit juice? Not me, and I am sure I speak for a great deal of the population when I say – there is just no way! Even if you can get past the ravenous hunger and the hectic headaches, nausea and dizziness, what on earth happens when you stop the fast? Well, if you are anything like me, you pig out and gain back what you lost as well as an extra pound or two for your trouble! It's just not worth it, mainly because it isn't sustainable.

For any diet to be effective, it has to be sustainable! I'm sure I'm not telling you anything new here. You KNOW diets, pills and potions that promise you will lose 10 pounds in a week are having you on. You know it, so why do we so often fall into the trap of believing all the marketing? Well, it's because people who want to lose weight are desperate for a quick fix, desperate to not have to live on carrot and celery sticks for months on end and desperate not to have to spend a major portion of their days staring at the same wall while running for miles on a treadmill! So desperate we are, that we will try anything in the hopes that "maybe this one works".

Well I am here to educate you on a lifestyle change that will transform you – mind, body and soul! No more forbidden foods. No more living on rabbit food. No more drinking your dinner. And most importantly, no more weight! I am going to introduce you to the *Fast Diet* – a revolutionary weight loss plan that works, is sustainable and can be backed up by science – now does that check all the boxes or what?

I'm a simple girl and the thing I like the most about the fast diet is that you are not bogged down by a ton of rules (only eat protein with veg and a little carbs, or is it no carbs and a little dairy?) – You quickly get confused and it becomes too much of an effort to maintain.

The fast diet is simplicity personified! It incorporates a practice called intermittent fasting, something that has been used by many cultures and religions for centuries. Basically the one and only rule of this diet is that you must fast for 2 non-consecutive days out of an entire week. For the other 5 days of the week, you can resume your normal eating patterns.

Now before you turn off your kindle or throw this book out of frustration at yet another starvation diet, hear me out. "Fasting" does not mean starving yourself – I cannot stress this enough! On your fast days you are simply limited in the calories you can consume. For men you have a 600 calorie limit and ladies, you get 500 calories. I know this seems like a paltry amount, but I promise you, once you get through reading the awesome recipes in this book and realize just how much you can actually do with 5/600 calories in a day, you will be converted.

Fasting and low calorie meals DO NOT mean you compromise on the flavor and quality of your meals – it simply means you need to allow your creative culinary juices to flow to prepare something more exciting than chicken breasts and boiled cabbage for 2 days. And believe you me, this book is choc-a-block with exciting, enticing, mouthwatering meals to keep you satiated from morning to night on your fast days.

The Science and Health Benefits of the Fast Diet

Not yet convinced? Let me tell you a bit more about the science behind this diet.

Healthy weight loss is rooted in common sense and that's the bottom line. As a general rule of thumb, if you lose it quickly, you will gain it back quickly. Because the fast diet allows you to enjoy your favorite foods and does not lock any food groups up in quarantine, it is much easier to sustain in the long term. Weight loss might be a bit slower, but it is steady and permanent. Not to mention your psychological well-being. How many of us spiral into self-hate and mentally flagellate and flog ourselves when we cheat on a diet (no matter how big or small the cheat is). We feel like a failure. Our already fragile self-esteem and self-worth takes yet another knock and eventually it just tears our confidence apart.

By making everything allowed, many people find their cravings for all the wrong things diminish. The only thing that banning a food does is to turn it into the most delicious forbidden temptation and you only want it all the more. Seriously, tell yourself you absolutely cannot eat chocolate and what will dominate every waking minute of your day until you scarf down an entire slab? Yup – CHOCOLATE!

With the fast diet, what you eat on non-fast days is entirely up to you – you can have your cake and eat it (and even lick the plate too if you like!). Now don't get me wrong, I am certainly not suggesting that you eat pizza for breakfast, cake for lunch and pies for dinner with an order of Mickey D's for a snack on the 5 off days (remember common sense). What it does mean is that should you feel like a "treat/cheat", you can have it without the accompanying guilt and without derailing your entire diet. The fast diet gives you the freedom to enjoy the favorite foods that you love (in moderation) while still sticking to your diet – just remember that with any freedom, comes responsibility!

The principles of dieting are simple – if you want to lose weight, simply consume less than your body utilizes. That way your body is forced to tap into the lush fat reserves on your dimpled thighs for energy and the result is weight loss. This whole process is called ketosis and it is this that helps you to lose fat and improves your body's ability to detox naturally.

The fast diet with its controlled intermittent fasting is not just about fitting into that pair of skinny jeans or sculpting a rocking bikini bod for the summer, it also boasts some truly impressive health benefits that should make you sit up and take notice. Scientific research has proven that there are definite and tangible benefits to the fast diet that go far beyond weight loss.

Intermittent fasting can transform not only your body, but your whole way of life. You will experience a shift in your attitude toward food and healthy food habits will begin to form naturally. Eating small meals throughout the day helps to boost your metabolism and keeps your body running optimally. You will enjoy improved mental and psychological health and an overall sense of well-being will settle over you. It has been shown that fasting actually helps to promote the growth of new nerve cells in the brain which is essential for memory, learning, focus and concentration. Furthermore, devotees have dubbed this the "happy diet" because they feel more positive, clear-headed and cheerful. The fast diet helps to lower blood pressure and cholesterol levels and accordingly reduces the risks associated with cardiac disease. It offers protection against neurodegenerative diseases like Alzheimer's and Parkinson's and has tentatively been shown to have positive links with cancer prevention.

Since regular meals help to stabilize blood sugar levels the fast diet plays a prominent role in staving off diabetes. Fasting has also been shown to redirect the body's energy consumption towards the immune system, strengthening it, which improves our ability to fight off diseases. The science doesn't lie and the facts speak for themselves.

Having said this, I would not be a responsible author if I did not issue a cautionary warning. This diet is not recommended for certain demographic groups. If you are diabetic, pregnant/breastfeeding, under 18 years of age, or have any other health concerns (like gastro-intestinal reflux) that require the regular intake of food to manage, you should not embark on this diet. And since good common sense is a recurring theme in this book, it is always a good idea to consult your doctor before embarking on any new diet/exercise regime.

Practical Tips to Keep You on Track

So you are still reading....that means you are serious about making a change, but now the big question – HOW? All this information can seem a little overwhelming at first, so here are some really useful practical tips to get you out of the starting blocks on the fast diet.

1. **As with anything fore planned is forewarned and a little pre planning goes a long way to ensure the smooth transition into this way of life.** It is best to plan your fast days in advance as well as the menu you are going to follow. Ensure that your kitchen is stocked with what you need before a fast day so you do not get tempted by last minute trips to the shops when you are having a reduced calorie day. NEVER shop on a fast day – unless you have steel resolve (which few of us do!). It is recommended to fast on days when you know you are going to busy, that way food is not foremost in your mind. Don't plan fast days on days when you know you have social engagements and if one should crop up unexpectedly you can change your fast day (fast days can be any 2 days that suit you, they do not have to be the same every week) – don't' set yourself up to fail, rather plan ahead to succeed!

2. On fast days you may utilize your calories as you see fit, so if that slice of pie looks good, you can have it, but it is going to be a long and hungry rest of the day. **Try to split your calories up evenly over the course of the day to stave off hunger.** Regular nutrition is what your body craves so give it what it needs! The delicious, creative recipes in this book will give you a great starting point for this. The more creative and tasty the food, the less it will feel like a diet and the easier it will be to stick to. Experiment with tastes, textures, herbs, spices and condiments – you never know, you may just hit on culinary gold!

3. **Try not to go on mad eating binges on your non-fast days.** Pigging out in preparation of a fast day is not the answer. You only stretch your stomach and end up feeling hungrier and all you ate the day before will simply be stored as fat anyway. The goal of this diet is to try and redefine your unhealthy relationship with food and set up healthier parameters instead. Being "forced" to think carefully about your food on fast days and becoming conscious of choosing foods that are more nutritionally sound is believed to lead to better food choices on non-fast days.

4. **HYDRATE!!!! Drink water...drink it often....drink a lot – the end!** Drinking water is crucial – it fills you up and is needed in the chemical reaction of burning fat. So

make sure you drink your 8 glasses. If you absolutely cannot stomach plain water, you can jazz it up with a bit of fresh lemon or other citrus juice, however you like it – just drink it! Hot lemon water is also a great between meal hunger-buster!

5. **Exercise is important for everyone, dieting or not, BUT you have to remember that on fast days your body is not going to be receiving enough fuel to handle long or strenuous workouts** – rather save those for the other 5 days and try to rest on fast days (most exercise programs recommend rest days anyway so it just takes a bit of planning to co-ordinate). For all you gym bunnies out there who absolutely have to be active, try a short brisk walk or something light on fast days. Also very important to remember is that exercise stimulates the appetite and you can feel especially hungry after a workout on a fast day and more likely to binge eat or exceed your calorie quota. Most of us are always complaining that we never have time to just smell the roses – well here is your excuse/reason/motivation – I hereby declare fast days rest days!

6. **Following from this, get enough shut-eye – sleep glorious sleep!!** Your ability to lose weight is seriously impeded when you are tired as sugary, starchy, calorie-laden comfort foods become infinitely more attractive!

7. **Make mealtimes an event** – just because you are eating smaller portions does not mean you have to hover shamefully in the kitchen, wolfing your meal down over the sink! Dish up your food and arrange it aesthetically on the plate. Pour a glass of water in a big wine glass and set the table. Eat slowly and chew your food well, while chatting with your family. If mealtimes remain enjoyable, the diet won't seem like a chore.

8. **If possible try to rope a friend, co-worker or partner into doing this diet with you.** It always helps to have someone who understands what you are going through first hand to support you through it.

9. **And finally, the biggie – stay off the scale!!!** We all know that weighing yourself everyday does nothing but depress you, but yet we all do it! There is far too much fluctuation with water retention and the like for an everyday weigh-in to be an accurate reflection of anything. Weekly weigh-ins are more than sufficient and a far more accurate reflection of weight loss. Try to weigh yourself at the same time every week (preferably in the morning, before breakfast). Try not to be discouraged by small losses – a loss is still a loss! Slow and steady weight loss is healthier and more permanent than losing a bunch of weight quickly.

Lastly, the number one rule of any diet (and in fact of life in general) is…. Be kind to yourself. Don't beat yourself up over perceived and imagined (self-decided) failures. You are only human and to err is natural! Stay positive and focused to the best of your ability. The first week of anything is always the hardest until you find your groove. Soon enough, this diet will fit seamlessly into your life and become second nature – something you do without thinking, like getting dressed in the mornings. Having said that – setbacks are a part of life and no matter how hard you try, there will be days when you just cannot resist an indulgent feast. When those happen, take them in your stride, be flexible and just start over the next day. This diet is not cast in stone. You are accountable to NO-ONE except yourself for your progress on it. So if you miss a fast day or eat more calories than you were supposed to, just pick up again the next day. Resume the plan and carry on. The fast diet is there to enhance your life, it is not meant to be a prison sentence. So get cooking, get your fast on and get out there and enjoy your life – it's the only one you have!

About the Recipes

A quick note about the wonderful recipes in this book; serving sizes are not listed for any of the recipes because *every* single recipe in this book serves 1! So there is no guesswork for you and no need to worry about serving sizes. ☺

Note that whenever you are using non-stick cooking spray, it is 7 calories per second! It may say 0 calories on the back of the can, but that is not accurate. I have incorporated the non-stick cooking spray calories into each recipe, but if you use more than what I advise, you will need to take those calories into account.

Also, in case you're wondering, whenever I refer to a 'dash' of something, technically speaking, a dash is 1/8 tsp. (Though if you're using salt you can use much more than a dash and still not affect the calorie count). If you decide to use more than a 'dash' of pepper however, then note that ground black pepper is 6 calories per teaspoon.

Now without further ado, onto the recipes! I have a feeling that you're going to *love* what I have in store.

BREAKFAST
Around 100 Calories

Egg in a Blanket

A quirky take on traditional bacon and eggs, these delicious prosciutto wrapped eggs are a great way to jump start your day! If you prefer a bit more of flavor kick, sprinkle on some red pepper flakes with the added bonus of a metabolism boost to get your system pumping for the day ahead.

Prep Time	:	10 minutes
Cook Time	:	10 – 15 minutes (depending on how you like your eggs)
Calories	:	**123**

Ingredients:

25g prosciutto	36 calories
1 large egg (50g)	72 calories
18g mushroom – thinly sliced	4 calories
¼ tsp paprika	2 calories
¼ tsp garlic powder	2 calories
Non-stick cooking spray (1 second)	7 calories

Method:

1. Spray 1 cup in a standard muffin tin with non-stick cooking spray (for 1 second).
2. Line the inside of the muffin cup with the prosciutto slice(s).
3. Now lay the thinly sliced mushrooms on the bottom of the muffin cup and sprinkle the garlic powder on top.
4. Crack the egg on top of the mushrooms and finish off with a dusting of paprika.
5. Bake for 10 – 15 minutes at 180° C or until the eggs are cooked to your preference.
6. Allow the egg parcel to cool slightly before removing it from the muffin tin.
7. Devour!

Funky Peach Raspberry Smoothie

Funky Peach Raspberry Smoothie

This delightful fruit smoothie blended with low fat yogurt and peachy undertones will make your taste buds sing! Not to mention it is incredibly filling! The raspberries and vanilla add a subtle flavorful depth and refreshing quality to transform your day from bland to extraordinary.

Prep Time	:	20 minutes
Cook Time	:	0 minutes
Calories	:	**157**

Ingredients:

✓ 112g plain low fat yogurt	55 calories
✓ 1 medium peach (150g) – chopped and pitted	59 calories
✓ 61g raspberries (or 1/2 cup)	32 calories
✓ ½ teaspoon sugar	8 calories
✓ ¼ teaspoon vanilla essence	3 calories
✓ Handful of ice cubes (optional)	0 calories

Method:

1. Place all the ingredients into the blender and pulse until smooth.
2. Pour into your serving glass and tuck in and enjoy!

*Note – For the fruit you may use fresh or frozen ingredients as long as they are unsweetened. You can also substitute the fruits seasonally or to taste. Just don't forget to check the calories!

Vanilla Oatmeal Waffle

Warm waffles in the morning are comfort food and this recipe does not disappoint. By using grinded dry oats as a substitute for flour we are able to reduce the overall calorie count, while not sacrificing even a bit on taste. The hint of vanilla ups the flavor ante making this a delicious and filling breakfast option. This recipe makes one medium sized waffle.

Prep Time	:	5 minutes
Cook Time	:	10 minutes
Calories	:	**168**

Ingredients:

27g regular or quick oatmeal, dry	102 calories
3/4 tsp baking powder	4 calories
1/4 cup (60g) unsweetened vanilla almond milk	8 calories
1 egg white	16 calories
1 tsp sugar	15 calories
1 tsp cinnamon	6 calories
1 tbsp unsweetened applesauce	7 calories
1/4 teaspoon vanilla	3 calories
Pinch of salt	0 calories
Non-stick cooking spray (1 second)	7 calories

Method:

1. To make the oats suitable as a flour substitute, take about 40g of dry oats and place in a blender or food processor and grind until it is the consistency of flour.
2. Scoop up 27g of the oat flour and place in a bowl. Freeze or refrigerate any left-over oat flour if you'd like.
3. Put the rest of the *dry* ingredients in the bowl and set the bowl aside.
4. In a separate bowl add your egg white, unsweetened vanilla almond milk, vanilla, and applesauce and whisk together.
5. Now mix the wet and dry ingredients together nicely.
6. Spray your waffle iron with some non-stick cooking spray (for 1 second) and pour the batter out to cook.
7. Cook until golden. Serve immediately.
8. Eat it up. YUM!

*Note – For a low calorie syrup alternative, use unsweetened applesauce at just 7 calories per tablespoon!

Tomato Stuffing Surprise

Tomato Stuffing Surprise

What a treat this is! Packed full of nutrition and flavor you will be full and ready to go after eating this. Although this meal takes a bit longer to cook it is totally worth the wait!

Prep Time	:	10 minutes
Cook Time	:	50 minutes
Calories	:	**144**

Ingredients:

1 large beefsteak tomato (about 180g)	32 calories
1 large egg (50g)	72 calories
2 tablespoons frozen corn	15 calories
1 tablespoon parmesan cheese – grated	22 calories
½ teaspoon chives – chopped	0 calories
¼ teaspoon garlic powder	2 calories
¼ teaspoon oregano	1 calorie
Salt and black pepper to taste	0 calories for a dash of each

Method:

1. Line a small baking dish with some parchment/greaseproof paper and preheat the oven to 180° C.
2. Slice the top off the tomato and use a melon baller or a spoon to gently hollow out the tomato. Discard the seeds and flesh.
3. Sprinkle the ¼ teaspoon of oregano onto the inside walls of the tomato.
4. Whisk the rest of the ingredients except the cheese together in a small jug and carefully pour the mixture into the hollowed out tomato.
5. Sprinkle the parmesan cheese evenly over the top.
6. Place the tomato onto the prepared baking dish and cook for 50 minutes or until the egg is set.
7. Allow to cool down slightly before serving.
8. Simply superb!

Sunrise Sweet and Spicy Salsa

Sunrise Sweet and Spicy Salsa

Rev your engine early with this spicy, fruity salsa breakfast. Not only does your body get a major boost of vitamins and minerals from the fruit, but adding a touch of chili powder kicks your metabolism into fat-busting gear. What a way to start your day!

Prep Time	:	20 minutes
Cook Time	:	0 minutes
Calories	:	**148**

Ingredients:

115g pineapple – chopped	57 calories
50g banana – peeled and chopped	45 calories
50g mango – chopped	35 calories
3g jalapeno pepper – seeds removed and diced	1 calorie
1 tablespoon red onion – finely diced	4 calories
1 tablespoon lime juice	4 calories
1 teaspoon freshly chopped coriander	0 calories
¼ teaspoon chili powder (or to taste)	2 calories

Method:

1. Chop up all the ingredients and place them in a bowl, tossing lightly to combine.
2. Add the lime juice over the top and then lightly dust the fruit with the chili powder.
3. Finish off with a sprinkle of finely chopped coriander.
4. Dig in and enjoy!

Toasted Almond Butter Fruit Spread

If you are looking for a healthy, filling and nutritious breakfast, look no further because this recipe ticks all the boxes! Crunchy toast smeared with smooth and creamy almond butter and topped with juicy fruit – the contrast of flavors and textures meld together into the perfect breakfast that can be thrown together in 5 minutes flat!

Prep Time	:	5 minutes
Cook Time	:	0 minutes
Calories	:	**156**

Ingredients:

1 slice light multi-grain bread	No more than 45 calories
50g banana – sliced thinly	45 calories
50g fresh blueberries	29 calories
1 teaspoon almond butter	34 calories
¼ teaspoon flax seeds	3 calories

Method:

1. Pop your bread in the toaster and cook it to your preference.
2. While the toast cooks, slice your banana and get the rest of the ingredients ready.
3. To assemble – spread the almond butter onto the toast and sprinkle the flax seeds on top, then lay the banana slices on top and finish off with the blueberries.
4. Absolutely scrumptious!

*For a delicious variation, try substituting apple slices for the bread and cinnamon for the flax seeds – YUM!

Hearty Home-style Hash Browns

Who says diet food has to be bland and boring? These hash browns are bursting with flavor and when topped with some delicious smoked salmon you cannot go wrong.

Prep Time	:	10 minutes
Cook Time	:	10 minutes
Calories	:	**154**

Ingredients:

75g potato – peeled and grated	58 calories
50g smoked salmon	59 calories
1 teaspoon or 5g mustard	3 calories
1 tablespoon onion – finely diced	4 calories
1 teaspoon flour	9 calories
1 teaspoon chives – chopped	0 calories
½ teaspoon minced garlic	2 calories
Dash Black pepper	0 calories
Non-stick cooking spray (2 seconds)	14 calories

Method:

1. Mix the grated potato, wholegrain mustard, flour, onion and garlic together in a bowl until they are well combined.
2. Divide the mixture into 2 equal portions, spray a non-stick pan with some cooking spray and heat it up over a medium heat.
3. Place the potato mixture into the pan and press it down flat with the back of a spoon.
4. Cook until both sides are nicely brown and the hash brown starts to get crispy.
5. Remove the hash browns from the pan and place them on a serving plate.
6. Top with the smoked salmon and garnish with the chopped chives and black pepper.
7. Totally amazing!

Ham and Spinach Egg Patty

Taking an unusual spin on your classic omelet, this is a breakfast you can whip up in 5 minutes flat! The triple protein power boost will rev you up and keep you happy until lunch!

Prep Time	:	less than 5 minutes
Cook Time	:	5 minutes
Calories	:	123

Ingredients:

2 egg whites – beaten	32 calories
25g ham – finely chopped	41 calories
25g spinach – shredded	6 calories
1 garlic clove – minced	4 calories
1 teaspoon olive oil	40 calories

Method:

1. Heat up the olive oil in a non-stick pan over a medium high heat and sauté the garlic clove for 1 minute until fragrant.
2. Add the spinach and ham and cook, stirring, until the spinach has wilted (no more than 2 minutes).
3. Pour in the beaten egg whites and leave them to set.
4. When the underside is brown, flip the patty over and brown the other side. It shouldn't take longer than about 1 minute per side.
5. Transfer the patty to your serving plate.
6. Gobble it up!

LUNCH
Around 100 Calories

Oriental Seared Tuna Salad

Oriental Seared Tuna Salad

This light lunch has a distinct Asian feel to it and packs a flavor punch. It can literally be thrown together in a few minutes and is the perfect on the go meal for those hectic busy days.

Prep Time	:	10 minutes
Cook Time	:	1 minute
Calories	:	**147**

Ingredients:

90g tuna steak – cut into strips	110 calories
50g rocket	13 calories
30g cherry tomatoes – cut in half	5 calories
1 tablespoon soy sauce	8 calories
1 teaspoon lime juice	1 calorie
½ teaspoon sesame seeds	9 calories
¼ teaspoon red pepper flakes	1 calorie

Method:

1. Mix the tuna and soy sauce together in a bowl and allow to marinate for 5 minutes while you prepare the salad.
2. Place the rocket in a bowl and top with the cherry tomatoes and red pepper flakes.
3. Heat a non-stick frying pan over a high heat and sear the tuna strips for about 20 seconds per side.
4. Place them on top of the salad and drizzle with lime juice.
5. Finish off with a garnish of sesame seeds.
6. Eat and enjoy!

Steak Pinwheels

These are delicious! Succulent steak stuffed with Dijon mustard and spinach, grilled to perfection and accompanied by a simple rocket salad makes this a tasty lunchtime treat that you will definitely make again and again.

Prep Time	:	10 minutes
Cook Time	:	20 minutes
Calories	:	**143**

Ingredients:

60g flank steak – pounded thin	116 calories
40g rocket	10 calories
25g baby spinach leaves	16 calories
1 tablespoon Dijon mustard	10 calories

Method:

1. Heat the grill to medium high
2. Cut the steak in half horizontally, but don't cut it all the way through. You need to be able to open it like a book.
3. Spread the Dijon mustard over the steak and top with the baby spinach leaves, then roll it up and tie it in place with cooking string.
4. Grill the steak for about 20 minutes – you can adjust the cooking time depending on how you like your steak cooked.
5. When the steak is cooked to your liking, remove it from under the grill and allow the meat to rest for 5 minutes before slicing it.
6. Serve the steak pinwheels with a side of fresh rocket.
7. Very moreish (unfortunately!)

Super Shroom Stroganoff

This delightful creamy dish is a winner any day of the week. Its filling, low in calories, easy to make and unbelievably tasty! Paprika adds a smoky undertone that is perfectly complemented by a subtle hint of garlic to make this a dish that stands out from the rest.

Prep Time	:	10 minutes
Cook Time	:	25 minutes
Calories	:	**126**

Ingredients:

125g mushrooms – chopped	27 calories
60ml vegetable stock	5 calories
1 celery stalk (40g) – sliced thin	3 calories
¼ onion (28g) – sliced thin	12 calories
1 garlic clove – minced	4 calories
2 tablespoons sour cream	51 calories
½ teaspoon olive oil	20 calories
½ teaspoon smoked paprika	3 calories
Dash of Black pepper	0 calories
1 tablespoon Freshly chopped parsley to garnish	1 calorie

Method:

1. Heat the oil in a non-stick pan over a medium heat, then add the celery, garlic and onions and cook until they are beginning to soften (about 5 minutes)
2. Add the chopped mushrooms and smoked paprika and cook for a further 5 minutes.
3. Pour in the vegetable stock and cook until the liquid reduces by half (about 10 minutes)
4. Stir in the sour cream and cook for a further 5 minutes.
5. Serve immediately and garnish with black pepper and chopped parsley.
6. Absolutely delicious!

Flavors of Fall Carrot Soup

Flavors of Fall Carrot Soup

Fall evokes a certain magic in the soul and nothing says fall like the colors orange and red and spicy cinnamon aromas. Tuck into this delicious soup when the temperature drops and revel in the comfort as you inhale and ingest the flavors of fall.

Prep Time	:	15 minutes
Cook Time	:	30 minutes
Calories	:	**141**

Ingredients:

128g carrots – peeled and roughly chopped	52 calories
250ml vegetable stock	22 calories
¼ onion (28g) – chopped	12 calories
1 garlic clove – minced	4 calories
1 teaspoon olive oil	40 calories
½ teaspoon grated ginger	3 calories
½ teaspoon cinnamon	3 calories
¼ teaspoon nutmeg	3 calories
¼ teaspoon allspice	1 calorie
¼ teaspoon red pepper flakes	1 calorie

Method:

1. Heat the olive oil in a non-stick saucepan over a medium heat and sauté the garlic and ginger for 1 minute, then add the onions and carrots and cook until they begin to soften.
2. Whisk in the rest of the ingredients except the red pepper flakes and bring the soup to a boil.
3. Cover the pot, reduce the heat and allow to simmer for 20 minutes.
4. Remove the pot from the heat and blend the soup using an immersion blender until smooth.
5. Serve with a sprinkle of red pepper flakes over the top.
6. Absolutely amazing – enjoy!

Grilled Cheese with a Beefy Twist

Adding meat to classic grilled cheese upgrades it from a snack to a meal and makes it an incredibly satisfying lunch to enjoy anytime. Add a dash of cayenne pepper if you like a bit of heat or simply enjoy it as is.

Prep Time	:	10 minutes
Cook Time	:	20 minutes
Calories	:	137

Ingredients:

1 slice light multi-grain bread	No more than 45 calories
40g of lean minced/ground beef (maximum 5% fat)	56 calories
1 tablespoon mozzarella cheese – grated	21 calories
½ tablespoon onion – finely chopped	2 calories
1 tablespoon tomato purée	13 calories
Dash cayenne pepper (optional)	0 calories

Method:

1. Pop the bread into the toaster and line a baking tray with foil.
2. Heat the oven up on the grill/broil setting.
3. Heat up a non-stick pan over a medium high heat and sauté the onions and beef until nicely browned.
4. Add the tomato purée and stir well to distribute it throughout the beef.
5. Place the piece of toast onto the baking tray and spread the beef in an even layer on top.
6. Sprinkle the grated mozzarella over the top and add the cayenne pepper if you are using it.
7. Place it under the grill/broiler until the cheese is bubbly and brown.
8. Allow to cool slightly before serving.

Island Style Chicken Wraps

This is an incredibly easy, yet tasty low calorie lunch that will have you dreaming of the beach with its prominent island flavors. The meat is succulent and cooked to perfection, then wrapped up in a crisp romaine lettuce leaf for a stark contrast in texture. A true gustatory gem!

Prep Time	:	15 minutes
Cook Time	:	10 minutes
Calories	:	**143**

Ingredients:

60g minced chicken	114 calories
125ml water	0 calories
¼ onion (28g) – finely diced	12 calories
1 tablespoon lime juice	4 calories
½ tablespoon fish sauce	3 calories
½ tablespoon freshly chopped coriander	0 calories
2 large leaves Romaine lettuce	10 calories

Method:

1. Wash and dry the romaine lettuce and place the leaves onto your serving plate
2. Cook the chicken and onion in the water until the chicken is no longer pink, breaking up any clumps that form as it cooks.
3. When the chicken is done, drain off any excess water and stir in the lime juice, fish sauce and freshly chopped coriander.
4. Spoon half the chicken mixture into each lettuce leaf, wrap it up and devour!
5. So tasty – enjoy!

Mint Watermelon Salad with Feta and Olives

Mint Watermelon Salad with Feta and Olives

This mint watermelon salad with olives is simplicity at its finest, but also a taste explosion. Subtle hints of lemon and mint complement the watermelon perfectly without overpowering the dish. Served with a bit of feta cheese, you will be hard pressed to find a tastier low calorie creation.

Prep Time	:	15 minutes
Cook Time	:	0 minutes
Calories	:	**159**

Ingredients:

228g watermelon – cubed	68 calories
22g feta cheese – drained and crumbled	58 calories
3 olives – sliced	15 calories
1 tbsp. red onion – chopped	4 calories
1 tsp lemon juice	1 calorie
16g mint leaves (or about 1/4 cup loosely packed)	7 calories
1 tsp pepper (optional)	6 calories
dash of salt (optional)	0 calories

Method:

1. Combine the watermelon and lemon juice in a bowl.
2. Add the feta cheese and very gently toss the feta cheese around until it lightly coats the watermelon.
3. Add the onions and sliced olives into the bowl.
4. Very, very finely chop up the mint leaves and toss it into the bowl.
5. Add the pepper and a bit of salt if you'd like.
6. Serve immediately.
7. To die for!

Heavenly Halibut with Broccoli Salad

Simple, elegant and unusual! A raw broccoli salad tossed with a lime, sesame and ginger dressing truly raises this dish to extraordinary heights and complements the delicious, uniquely flavored fish perfectly.

Prep Time	:	10 minutes
Cook Time	:	20 minutes
Calories	:	**148**

Ingredients:

✓ 85g halibut fillet	94 calories
✓ 40g fresh broccoli – cut into small florets	14 calories
✓ 1 tablespoon red onion – finely chopped	4 calories
✓ 1 tablespoon spring onions - chopped	5 calories
✓ 1 tablespoon lime juice	4 calories
✓ ½ teaspoon grated ginger	3 calories
✓ ¼ teaspoon sesame seeds	4 calories
✓ 1 tbsp. fat free sour cream	9 calories
✓ ½ tbsp. grated parmesan cheese	10 calories
✓ Dash of garlic powder	1 calorie
✓ Dash of salt and pepper	0 calories

Method:

1. Preheat oven to 190°C. Season the thawed fish with a little salt and pepper.
2. In a small bowl, mix the sour cream, parmesan cheese, and garlic powder.
3. Spread the mixture over the fish and place fish in the oven for about 20 minutes, or until fish is firm.
4. While the fish cooks prepare the salad. Place the broccoli and *red* onions in a bowl and toss to combine.
5. Mix the lime juice, ginger and sesame seeds together and pour the mixture over the broccoli, tossing to coat the florets well.
6. Top the fish with the spring onions, serve with broccoli salad, and enjoy!

DINNER
Around 100 Calories

Faux Veggie Pasta

Pasta is many a person's diet weakness, so this recipe satisfies those cravings for starchy carbs by using courgette noodles as "pasta". Tossed with a colorful combination of crunchy fresh vegetables, this dish is a nutritious and tasty dinner option.

Prep Time	:	15 minutes
Cook Time	:	15 minutes
Calories	:	**147**

Ingredients:

1 courgette (180g)	31 calories
1 red pepper (110g) – cut into thin strips	37 calories
½ an onion (56g) – sliced thin	24 calories
50g mushrooms – sliced thin	11 calories
1 garlic clove – minced	4 calories
1 teaspoon olive oil	40 calories

Method:

1. Use a peeler to slice the courgette into thin ribbons, then set aside in a bowl.
2. Heat the olive oil in a non-stick pan over a medium heat and sauté the onion and garlic for 1 minute.
3. Add the red pepper and cook until it begins to soften and then add the mushrooms.
4. When the mushrooms are tender, stir in the courgette "pasta" and cook until it is warm throughout.
5. The courgette cooks very quickly, so you need to keep a close eye on it so it does not turn mushy.
6. Serve while hot and enjoy!

Baby Aubergine Stew

Baby Aubergine Stew

Strong Middle Eastern flavors are the signature of this spicy hearty stew. This one pot meal is super-healthy, high in fiber and low in calories. A must-try meal!

Prep Time	:	10 minutes
Cook Time	:	45 minutes
Calories	:	**148**

Ingredients:

300g baby aubergines – whole with the stalk in tact	73 calories
100g chopped tomatoes	18 calories
½ red onion (56g) – chopped	24 calories
1 garlic clove – minced	4 calories
1 serrano or jalapeno pepper– seeds removed and sliced thinly	4 calories
1 teaspoon freshly chopped mint	1 calorie
½ teaspoon coriander seeds	0 calories
½ teaspoon cumin seeds	4 calories
½ teaspoon olive oil	20 calories

Method:

1. Heat up the olive oil in a pot over a medium heat, add the onions and garlic and cook until they begin to brown, then add the cumin seeds, chili and coriander seeds.
2. When the seeds become fragrant, place the aubergines into the pot and coat them in the onion mixture.
3. Add the tomatoes and stir to combine.
4. Cover the pot and cook for about 40 minutes or until the aubergines are tender.
5. Just before serving, stir in the freshly chopped mint.
6. Enjoy this hearty stew while it's hot!

Salmon and Asparagus Bake

Salmon and Asparagus Bake

This delightfully simple dish is a filling and appetizing dinner to enjoy anytime. The lemon not only keeps the fish succulent and provides an incredible "zing" to the end flavor, but also kicks your body into detox mode with its incredible fat busting properties.

Prep Time	:	10 minutes
Cook Time	:	30 minutes
Calories	:	**142**

Ingredients:

85g salmon fillet (chinook)	100 calories
75g asparagus spears – ends trimmed	15 calories
1 lemon (58g) – thinly sliced	17 calories
½ tablespoon freshly chopped dill	4 calories
1 tsp ground black pepper	6 calories
Salt to taste	0 calories

Method:

1. Lay the asparagus spears out in a single layer on the bottom of a shallow baking dish.
2. Season the salmon with salt and pepper, and place the salmon fillet on top of the asparagus and cover with the lemon slices.
3. Cover the baking dish tightly with foil and pop it into the oven at 180° C for 30 minutes.
4. Serve with the freshly chopped dill sprinkled on top.
5. Gobble it up!

4 Ingredient Chicken Curry

A tasty chicken curry under 150 calories? Who would have thought that was possible? Well, here it is folks and with only 4 ingredients, it does not get easier to make. Simple and totally scrumptious, now that's a top recipe in my books!

Prep Time   :   Under 5 minutes
Cook Time   :   30 minutes

Calories   :   **140**

Ingredients:

50g chicken breast – cut into cubes	82 calories
60 ml milk – 2% fat or less	31 calories
1 teaspoon red curry paste	20 calories
1 teaspoon finely chopped coriander	0 calories
Non-stick cooking spray (1 second)	7 calories

Method:

1. Spray a saucepan with a little non-stick cooking spray and gently brown the chicken pieces over a medium heat.
2. While the chicken cooks, whisk the curry paste into the milk.
3. Pour the curried milk over the chicken pieces and allow to simmer for 15 – 20 minutes.
4. Serve with some chopped coriander as a garnish.
5. Delicious!

Grilled Chipotle Lime Shrimp

Savory shrimp grilled and paired perfectly with some chipotle lime marinade. The combination of fiery chipotle offsets the tartness of the lime beautifully and creates a taste sensation second to none.

Prep Time	:	10 minutes
Cook Time	:	5 minutes
Calories	:	**125**

Ingredients:

12 medium shrimp (83g)	84 calories
1 small chipotle chili (from a can of chiles in adobo) - chopped	10 calories
1 tsp adobo sauce (from a can of chiles in adobo)	3 calories
1 lime (67g), juice and zest	20 calories
1 garlic clove, chopped	5 calories
½ tsp cumin	3 calories
Salt to taste	0 calories
Dash of pepper	0 calories

Method:

1. Mix all of the ingredients (minus the shrimp) into a bowl.
2. Marinate the shrimp into the mixture for at least 20 minutes.
3. Skewer the shrimp and grill on medium-high heat for about 2 minutes per side.
4. Dig in!

Raw Veggie and Chicken Tortilla
48

Raw Veggie and Chicken Tortilla

This is an incredibly healthy and filling dinner. Crammed full of raw veggies you are guaranteed and vitamin and antioxidant boost and adding chicken means you get a serving of protein too. Easy and quick to prepare with a terrific taste – you cannot go wrong with this one!

Prep Time	:	15 minutes
Cook Time	:	0 minutes
Calories	:	**141**

Ingredients:

1 flour tortilla (24g)	52 calories
25g boneless, skinless chicken – cooked and sliced (this is a great recipe to use up any left overs)	30 calories
40g romaine lettuce – shredded	6 calories
20g carrots – julienned	8 calories
20g cucumber – julienned	3 calories
20g celery – julienned	3 calories
20g bean sprouts	6 calories
2 spring onions (30g) – chopped	10 calories
1 tablespoon hummus	23 calories
1 tablespoon freshly chopped coriander	0 calories

Method:

1. Lay the tortilla onto a plate and spread the hummus over it in an even layer.
2. Mix the rest of the ingredients together in a bowl and lay them down the center of the tortilla.
3. Wrap the tortilla up around the ingredients.
4. Munch Munch Munch!

So Simple Scallops & Salsa

So Simple Scallops & Salsa

Seafood is delicious – fact! And when it's quick and easy to prepare the taste factor seems to be even better. You cannot beat 6 ingredients and a 10 minute cooking time and what is saved in time seems to be made up for in taste – these scallops are simply bursting with flavor!

Prep Time	:	5 minutes
Cook Time	:	10 minutes
Calories	:	**147**

Ingredients:

105g scallops	117 calories
1 teaspoon garlic powder	9 calories
½ teaspoon chili powder	4 calories
1 tablespoon lemon juice	4 calories
21g pineapple chunks -diced	11 calories
5g jalapeno pepper	2 calories

Method:

1. Place the scallops in a bowl and squeeze over the lemon juice.
2. Sprinkle on the spices and toss well to coat.
3. Place the spiced scallops on a baking tray under the broiler for 5 minutes per side.
4. Mix the pineapple chunks and jalapeno pepper in a bowl.
5. Top the salsa over the scallops.
6. Serve immediately and enjoy!

*Note – these can be a stand-alone meal, but if you prefer some veggies to accompany the scallops, simply reduce the amount of scallops and substitute in some greens, but be sure to check your calories!

Super Speedy Vegetarian Soup

This belly warming soup is food for the soul! Jam packed with veggies and noodles it promises to leave you happy and satiated. Taking just 10 minutes to cook, this is the perfect meal for those rushed lunch times.

Prep Time	:	Less than 5 minutes
Cook Time	:	10 minutes
Calories	:	**158**

Ingredients:

250ml vegetable stock	22 calories
100g chopped tomatoes	18 calories
50g frozen mixed vegetables	33 calories
25g spaghetti – broken into short lengths	72 calories
1 teaspoon oregano	5 calories
1 teaspoon parmesan cheese – grated	8 calories

Method:

1. Bring the stock, oregano and tomatoes to a boil in a saucepan and then add the spaghetti lengths.
2. Cook for about 5 minutes and then add the frozen vegetables.
3. Cook for a further 5 minutes until the pasta and vegetables are soft.
4. Transfer to your serving bowl and top with some grated parmesan before serving.
5. Quick, easy and delicious – what more could you ask for?

Flavorsome Fiery Fish Parcel

This fish is steamed to perfection inside a foil parcel. Fabulously flavorsome and extremely simple to prepare, this fish dinner will fill your tummy and delight your palate – just be sure to have a big glass of water on hand!

Prep Time	:	10 minutes
Cook Time	:	15 minutes
Calories	:	**139**

Ingredients:

100g Haddock fillet	90 calories
25g pak choi – thinly sliced	3 calories
1 spring onion (15g) – chopped	5 calories
5g red chili – seeds removed and thinly sliced	16 calories
2g ginger – grated	7 calories
1 tbsp lime juice	4 calories
1 tablespoon water	0 calories
½ tablespoon soy sauce	4 calories
¼ teaspoon sesame oil	10 calories

Method:

1. Place the fish into the middle of a piece of heavy foil and top with the pak choi, spring onions, ginger and red chili.
2. Mix the rest of the ingredients together in a bowl and pour over the fish.
3. Pull up the edges of the foil and crimp them together to seal up the parcel, making sure there are no gaps for the steam to escape.
4. Place the foil parcel on a baking tray and bake in the oven at 180° C for 15 minutes.
5. When the fish is done, open the foil up very carefully as the steam is incredibly hot and will burn you.
6. Serve immediately and enjoy!

BREAKFAST
Around 200 Calories

Ultimate Breakfast Nachos

Nachos for breakfast? Why Not? A baked egg nestled into some cheesy spinach with tomatoes and baked tortilla chips – what's not to like? This vegetarian meal is easily upgraded to a meaty dish by simply adding a bit of bacon.

Prep Time	:	10 minutes
Cook Time	:	20-30 minutes
Calories	:	**239**

Ingredients:

5 baked tortilla crisps/chips (10g)	37 calories
3 cherry tomatoes (45g) – halved	9 calories
1 large egg (50g)	72 calories
57g baby spinach	13 calories
2 teaspoons lemon juice	4 calories
50g non-fat mozzarella cheese – shredded	71 calories
28g onion – diced	12 calories
Non-stick cooking spray – 3 seconds	21 calories
Dash of salt and black pepper	0 calories

Method:

1. Spray the non-stick cooking spray in a small pan and add the onions and sauté until they begin to soften.
2. Add the spinach and lemon juice and cook until the spinach has wilted.
3. While the veggies cook, arrange the tortilla crisps/chips in an oven safe pan and top with half the spinach mixture.
4. Sprinkle on the shredded cheese and then put the rest of the spinach mixture on top.
5. Now make a well in the middle of the pan and crack the egg in the hole.
6. Place the cherry tomato halves around the edge of the pan and season with salt and pepper.
7. Place the pan in the oven and bake at 180° C for 15 minutes or until the egg whites have set. If you do not like runny yolks, bake for longer.
8. Dig in! Nom, Nom, Nom!

Pumpkin Pie Smoothie

Pumpkin Pie Smoothie

Packed full of goodness, this is an awesome way to start your day. The perfect blend of cinnamon, nutmeg and pumpkin pie spice complements the creamy pumpkin puree and the granola adds some unexpected texture. Pumpkin pie in a glass – get yours!

Prep Time	:	10 minutes
Cook Time	:	0 minutes
Calories	:	**191**

Ingredients:

125ml milk – 2% fat or less	64 calories
125ml pumpkin puree	44 calories
4 tablespoons granola	70 calories
½ teaspoon vanilla essence	6 calories
½ teaspoon cinnamon	3 calories
¼ teaspoon freshly grated nutmeg	3 calories
¼ teaspoon pumpkin pie spice	1 calorie
Handful of ice cubes	0 calories

Method:

1. Place all the ingredients into the food processor and blend to your desired consistency.
2. Top with some cinnamon to serve.
3. It doesn't get easier than this!

*Note – while this is already low in calories, you could further limit your calorie intake by using unsweetened vanilla almond milk. Unsweetened vanilla almond milk will reduce the calorie intake of this incredible smoothie by 48 calories, for a total of 143 calories!

Gourmet Ricotta Honey Toast

Dine like royalty with this gourmet toast topping. Goat cheese, walnuts and pears topped with a sprinkling of cinnamon and finished off with a drizzle of honey. Sweet and savory, smooth and crunchy – a wonderful contradiction in flavor and texture that blends together in a complementary manner to make this a delightful and filling meal.

Prep Time	:	15 minutes
Cook Time	:	0 minutes
Calories	:	**211**

Ingredients:

1 slice light multi-grain bread , toasted	No more than 45 calories
30g or 2 tbsp ricotta cheese	53 calories
½ small pear (74g) – sliced *very* thinly	43 calories
1 tablespoon walnuts – roughly chopped	48 calories
1 teaspoon raw honey	21 calories
¼ teaspoon cinnamon	1 calorie
Dash of salt and pepper	0 calories

Method:

1. Spread the ricotta cheese on top of the toast, then add the chopped walnuts.
2. Lay the pear slices on top and sprinkle them with the cinnamon.
3. Finish off with a drizzle of honey.
4. Absolute glorious decadence – enjoy!

*Note – You can further reduce the calorie count by using part skim ricotta cheese and save yourself 11 calories, for a total of 200 calories!

Eggless Veggie Burrito

These breakfast burritos are packed full of a flavorful but light meat and veggie filling that will not weigh you down first thing. Spice them up with a pinch of cayenne pepper for an extra kick or simply enjoy them as is.

Prep Time	:	10 minutes
Cook Time	:	5 minutes
Calories	:	**235**

Ingredients:

1 corn tortilla (about 6 inch diameter, 24g)	52 calories
45g ham – diced	73 calories
50g mushrooms – sliced	11 calories
50g onion – diced	21 calories
50g red pepper – thinly sliced	16 calories
50g green pepper – thinly sliced	10 calories
1 tablespoon cheddar cheese – shredded	28 calories
Non-stick cooking spray – 3 seconds	21 calories
2 teaspoons salsa	3 calories

Method:

1. Spray the non-stick cooking spray in a small pan and add all the chopped ingredients.
2. Cook, stirring frequently for about 5 minutes and then remove from the heat.
3. Heat up the tortilla in the microwave for about 20 seconds.
4. Load the tortilla with the ham and veggie mixture, top with the shredded cheese and salsa and serve immediately.
5. Totally moreish!

Puffy Peach Drop Scone

Puffy Peach Drop Scone

This dish is nothing short of an aesthetic delight! Take it straight from the oven to the table and tuck into the scrumptious golden drop scone topped with sweet juicy peaches. A tasty treat to enjoy any day of the week.

Prep Time	:	10 minutes
Cook Time	:	25 minutes
Calories	:	**212**

Ingredients:

1 firm, ripe peach (130g) – pitted, peeled and diced	51 calories
1 egg white	16 calories
2 tablespoons flour	57 calories
2 tablespoons milk – 2% fat (or less)	15 calories
1 tablespoon brown sugar	34 calories
1 teaspoon lemon juice	1 calorie
1 teaspoon cinnamon	6 calories
1 teaspoon nutmeg	11 calories
Non-stick cooking spray – 3 seconds	21 seconds

Method:

1. Place the chopped peaches into a microwave safe bowl and microwave, uncovered, on high power until peach is tender, (3-5 minutes). Combine them with the sugar and lemon juice, then set aside.
2. Beat the egg white in a large bowl until it is light and fluffy, then stir in the flour and milk.
3. Keep beating until you get a smooth batter and then add half the cinnamon and stir well to mix.
4. Heat a skillet over medium-low heat and spray with your non-stick cooking spray (for 3 seconds). Add batter and cook the drop scone for 2-3 minutes on each side or until bubbles start to form and it is puffy and golden brown.
5. Remove from the skillet, top with the chopped peaches and sprinkle over the remaining cinnamon and nutmeg.
6. Serve immediately.

Cream Cheese Breakfast Bundles

Prepare yourselves for the most amazingly awesome and unique breakfast EVER! This one takes a bit more time to prepare, but every minute is totally worth it! The only downside is that you are going to want more!

Prep Time	:	30 minutes + 45 minutes chilling time
Cook Time	:	15 minutes
Calories	:	**252**

Ingredients:

1 medium egg (about 44g)	70 calories
40ml unsweetened vanilla almond milk	5 calories
30g fresh raspberries	16 calories
30g low fat cottage cheese	27 calories
30g low fat cream cheese	29 calories
2 tablespoons flour	57 calories
1 teaspoon butter – melted	34 calories
Non-stick cooking spray – 2 seconds	14 calories

Method:

1. Mix the milk, eggs, flour and butter together into a smooth batter, cover it and place it into the fridge for 45 minutes to chill.
2. When the time is up, spray a non-stick pan (1 second) with some cooking spray and heat it up over a medium heat.
3. Stir the refrigerated batter and then drop 2 tablespoons of the batter into the middle of the hot pan.
4. Tilt the pan to swirl the batter around so a thin crepe forms.
5. When the bottom is turning lightly golden, flip it over and cook the other side, then place on a wire rack to cool.
6. Repeat with the remaining batter.
7. Allow the crepes to cool for a few minutes while you make the filling.
8. Simply stir the cottage cheese and cream cheese together until smooth.
9. Now lay out your crepes and divide the cheese mixture between them, spreading it out into an even layer.
10. Fold opposite sides of the crepe over to meet, forming a bundle around the filling.
11. Place the bundles seam side down on a baking tray that has been lightly sprayed with cooking spray (1 second).
12. Bake for about 10 minutes in the oven at 180° C, or until they are golden brown and the filling is heated through.
13. Serve topped with fresh raspberries for an incredible breakfast treat!

*Remember – It is 7 calories for each additional second you spray the non-stick cooking spray, so be careful and only spray what you will need.

Kiwi and Strawberry Parfait

64

Kiwi and Strawberry Parfait

Layers of juicy fruit, crunchy cornflakes and smooth, creamy yogurt, this is not only a treat for your taste buds but it looks amazing too – almost too good to eat! This is a real time-save breakfast, taking under 10 minutes to prepare (and even less to eat I'll bet)!

Prep Time	:	Under 10 minutes
Cook Time	:	0 minutes
Calories	:	**231**

Ingredients:

240g low fat Greek style yogurt	141 calories
1 kiwi fruit (74g) – sliced	46 calories
4 strawberries (48g) – sliced	15 calories
8g cornflakes	29 calories

Method:

1. Simply layer the ingredients into a fancy glass in the following order: yogurt, strawberries, yogurt, kiwi, cornflakes, yogurt, cornflakes, strawberries, and kiwi.
2. Eat it up, it's delicious!

Apple Cinnamon Quinoa

Quinoa is one of those amazing super foods that can be eaten at any time of the day. This porridge takes your classic oatmeal and pairs it with some delicious fresh apples and red quinoa for something unique and tasty.

Prep Time	:	5 minutes
Cook Time	:	40 minutes
Calories	:	**221**

Ingredients:

1/2 apple (91g) – pitted, peeled and sliced	48 calories
40g red quinoa	76 calories
300ml water	0 calories
118ml unsweetened vanilla almond milk	15 calories
20g rolled oats	76 calories
1 teaspoon cinnamon	6 calories

Method:

1. Place the water, quinoa and apples into a saucepan and cook gently over a medium heat for 30 minutes.
2. Add the milk and oats and cook for 10 minutes or until the oats are soft.
3. Make sure you stir the porridge while it is cooking so that it does not stick to the saucepan.
4. Serve hot!
5. Belly warming soul food!

LUNCH
Around 200 Calories

Grilled Corn and Avocado Salad

Grilled Corn and Avocado Salad

An ear of corn, grilled to golden perfection, tossed with avocado slices, tomatoes, lime juice and chili pepper – you cannot go wrong with this as a healthy lunch. For a metabolism booster, add a dash of cayenne pepper to turn up the heat.

Prep Time	:	15 minutes
Cook Time	:	20 minutes
Calories	:	**255**

Ingredients:

1 large ear of yellow corn (118g)	127 calories
41g avocado – chopped	84 calories
½ red chili pepper (23g) - chopped	9 calories
4 cherry tomatoes (68g) - halved	12 calories
2 teaspoons lime juice	2 calories
2 tablespoons freshly chopped coriander	0 calories
½ teaspoon olive oil	20 calories
¼ teaspoon cayenne pepper	1 calorie

Method:

1. Heat up the grill to a medium high setting and chargrill the corn, turning often. This should take about 15 – 20 minutes.
2. While this cooks, mix the lime juice, coriander, and olive oil together.
3. When the corn is cooked, carefully cut the kernels off the cob and place them in a bowl.
4. Top with the chopped avocado, cherry tomatoes and red chili pepper and pour over the lime dressing.
5. Finish off with a sprinkling of cayenne pepper.
6. Dig in!

*Note – If you'd like to make this an even more filling lunch, then add some kidney beans. But be careful, kidney beans are 14 calories for each tbsp.

Tilapia with Jalapeno Coconut Relish

This tender flaky fish literally melts in your mouth. Seasoned to perfection and served with an exotic relish, this meal provides a superb taste sensation not to be missed.

Prep Time	:	10 minutes
Cook Time	:	15 minutes
Calories	:	**216**

Ingredients:

90g tilapia fillet	115 calories
¼ teaspoon minced garlic	1 calorie
2 teaspoons Italian seasoning	0 calories
Salt to taste	0 calories
½ cup diced cucumber (65g) – peeled	8 calories
21g desiccated coconut	74 calories
18g or 5 tbsp. chopped fresh chives	5 calories
1 tablespoon mint – finely chopped	3 calories
1 tablespoon coriander - chopped	0 calories
1 jalapeno pepper (14g)- minced	4 calories
1 tablespoon lime juice	4 calories
¼ teaspoon ground cumin	2 calories

Method:

1. Preheat oven to 220 °C and place the tilapia on a pan. Sprinkle over the garlic, Italian seasoning, and salt.
2. Bake the fish for 15 minutes or until it flakes easily with a fork.
3. To make the relish combine the remaining ingredients in a bowl and toss.
4. Serve with the delicious exotic relish. Soo delicious!

Tangy Chicken and Broccoli Pan

A tangy spin on classic chicken and broccoli stir-fry. Adding a bit of Dijon mustard and a splash of soy sauce really livens up an otherwise bland dish and makes this an extraordinary lunch to enjoy every day.

Prep Time	:	10 minutes
Cook Time	:	30 minutes
Calories	:	**248**

Ingredients:

100g chicken breasts – sliced	190 calories
75g broccoli – cut into florets	26 calories
60ml chicken stock	2 calories
2 teaspoon Dijon mustard	7 calories
1 teaspoon soy sauce	3 calories
½ teaspoon olive oil	20 calories

Method:

1. Heat up the olive oil in a non-stick pan over a medium high heat and cook the broccoli until tender crisp.
2. Remove from the pan and set aside for later.
3. Add the chicken pieces to the pan and sauté until they start to turn golden brown.
4. Mix the soy sauce and the chicken stock together and add it to the chicken in the pan.
5. Bring it to a boil and then reduce the heat and stir in the mustard.
6. Place the broccoli back in the pan and heat through gently before serving.
7. Serve and enjoy. YUMMY!

Tropical Spring Rolls with Vanilla Honey

This fruity delight will make your taste buds sing! Bright, colorful, juicy tropical fruits lovingly wrapped up in light rice paper and dipped into an amazing vanilla honey dipping sauce – well, it just doesn't get better than that!

Prep Time : 20 minutes
Cook Time : 0 minutes

Calories : 259

Ingredients:

2 rice paper wrappers (about 6-3/8" diameter)	40 calories
50g strawberries – sliced	16 calories
50g kiwi – chopped	31 calories
50g banana – chopped	45 calories
50g mango – julienned	35 calories
1 tablespoon freshly chopped mint	3 calories
28g honey	85 calories
¼ teaspoon vanilla essence	3 calories
1 teaspoon lime zest	1 calorie

Method:

*Note – the rice paper can be tricky to work with. I found it easier to double wrap the fruit so I only got 1 spring roll from the ingredients, but if you are able to use a single wrapper, you will get 2 rolls.

1. Fill a bowl with warm water and quickly dip the rice paper into it, remove it and pat it dry with a paper towel.
2. Add the second paper directly on top of the first.
3. Layer the fruit on top of the rice paper in the middle and sprinkle the chopped mint on top.
4. Now carefully fold up the bottom of the rice paper and tuck it under the fruit, fold in the sides and then roll it up to the end.
5. The wrap will seal itself as it will still be damp from the water.
6. To make the dipping sauce, combine the lime zest, vanilla and honey together in a bowl.
7. Dip the fruit stuffed spring roll into the sauce and devour!
8. Very addictive!

Chilled Cucumber & Radish Soup

Chilled Cucumber & Radish Soup

The cucumber is a humble, unassuming vegetable but takes center stage in this wonderful recipe, with their delicate, fresh flavor as the highlight. When served chilled, this soup is not only light, but completely refreshing – the perfect summers day lunch. This recipe is best if you make it ahead of time to allow it to chill.

Prep Time	:	20 minutes
Cook Time	:	0 minutes
Calories	:	**224**

Ingredients:

500g cucumber – seedless, peeled, and cut into chunks	77 calories
1 large radish (9g) - thinly sliced or chopped	1 calorie
130g nonfat greek yogurt	75 calories
1 tablespoon jalapeno – chopped and stem removed	2 calories
1 tablespoon red onion – roughly chopped	4 calories
water (optional)	0 calories
½ tablespoon olive oil	60 calories
½ tablespoon lemon juice (optional)	2 calories
½ garlic clove (1.5g) - minced	3 calories
Dash of salt and pepper	0 calories

Method:

1. Place all the ingredients except the radish into the food processor and blend until very smooth. If you prefer, add a little water little by little until you achieve your desired consistency, (though I usually don't).
2. Transfer to a clean bowl and place in the fridge for at least 2 hours to chill, but preferably overnight.
3. Place the soup in the freezer for 30 minutes prior to serving.
4. Top with the sliced/chopped radish.
5. Serve chilled and enjoy!
6. Amazing!

Sweet and Spicy Shrimp Pawpaw Wraps

These wraps are simply to die for! Scrumptious shrimp paired with pawpaw and jalapenos give kick the recipe up a notch. Quick, easy and tasty – convenience at its best. This recipe keeps calories in check by wrapping the shrimp up in Romaine lettuce leaves, rather than tortillas, but the end result is still finger-licking good!

Prep Time	:	10 minutes
Cook Time	:	0 minutes
Calories	:	**220**

Ingredients:

160g shrimp– peeled, deveined, and cut into bite size pieces	170 calories
75g pawpaw – peeled and cut into cubes	29 calories
2 large Romaine lettuce leaves	3 calories
2 tablespoons lime juice	8 calories
2 tablespoons coriander – finely chopped	0 calories
2 tablespoons spring onions – chopped	4 calories
2 teaspoons finely chopped jalapeno pepper	1 calorie
1 teaspoon balsamic vinegar	1 calorie
¼ teaspoon minced garlic	1 calorie
¼ teaspoon brown sugar (optional)	3 calories

Method:

1. Cook your shrimp by either boiling or grilling (depending on your preference).
2. Mix the shrimp and pawpaw together in a bowl.
3. Wash and dry the lettuce and set it aside for later.
4. Mix the remaining ingredients together in a separate bowl and pour the mixture over the pawpaw and shrimp.
5. Toss the ingredients together gently and ensure that they are well coated.
6. Divide the mixture between the lettuce leaves, roll it up and pig out!

Tomato and Mushroom Baked Salmon

This one dish meal is quick to prepare and packs a flavor punch. Throw it all in a baking dish, pop it in the oven and forget about it – now that's my kind of meal!

Prep Time	:	10 minutes
Cook Time	:	30 minutes
Calories	:	**247**

Ingredients:

150g salmon fillet	198 calories
30g baby spinach leaves	7 calories
1 tablespoon lemon juice	4 calories
50g mushrooms – sliced	11 calories
50g tomato – diced	9 calories
½ teaspoon black pepper	3 calories
¼ teaspoon minced garlic	1 calorie
Non-stick cooking spray – 2 seconds	14 calories

Method:

1. Spray a baking dish with some cooking spray and place the salmon in it skin side down.
2. Sprinkle the black pepper over the salmon to season.
3. Mix the rest of the ingredients together except for the lemon juice and spoon them over the piece of salmon.
4. Squeeze some lemon juice over everything, then place the baking dish into the oven and bake at 180° C for 30 minutes or until the fish flakes easily with a fork.
5. Tuck in and enjoy – superb!

Beef Stir-Fry in the Blink of an Eye

Beef Stir-Fry in the Blink of an Eye

Nothing beats a hearty filling meal that can be whipped up fast. Not everyone has time for leisurely lunches and that's when we end up falling off the diet bandwagon. With recipes such as this you will never have to cheat again!

Prep Time	:	10 minutes
Cook Time	:	20 minutes
Calories	:	**239**

Ingredients:

58g sirloin steak, lean only – sliced into strips	139 calories
125ml beef stock	9 calories
40g asparagus – cut into pieces	8 calories
40g mushrooms – sliced	9 calories
40g red pepper – julienned	12 calories
1 tablespoon soy sauce	8 calories
1 teaspoon corn starch	12 calories
1 teaspoon olive oil	40 calories
½ teaspoon minced garlic	2 calories

Method:

1. Whisk the soy sauce, stock and corn starch together and set aside.
2. Heat the olive oil in a non-stick pan and add the garlic.
3. Cook the garlic for 2 minutes over a medium high heat and then add the beef strips and cook until they are brown.
4. Now add the veggies and cook until they are tender crisp.
5. Now pour over the stock mixture and allow it to come to a boil.
6. Reduce the heat and let simmer for 10 minutes for the sauce to thicken up.
7. Absolutely scrumptious!

*Note – Broil or grill your steak instead and you will further reduce your total calorie count to just 210 calories.

Fruity Corn Salsa with Citrus Dressing

A fruiter and more refreshing version of the 'Grilled Corn and Avocado Salad", you're sure to fall in love with this one just as much, if not even more! Light, low in calories and an absolute taste sensation! Savory vegetables, combined with sweet fruits and marinated in a tri-citrus dressing –your taste buds will thank you for days! Quick and easy to prepare, this is a real go-to lunch when you are rushed.

Prep Time	:	15 minutes
Cook Time	:	0 minutes
Calories	:	**227**

Ingredients:

1 large ear of yellow corn (118g) – grilled and cut off the cob	127 calories
1 medium peach (150g) – peeled, pitted and chopped	59 calories
30g mango– chopped	21 calories
60g tomato – chopped	11 calories
1 tablespoon red onion – chopped	4 calories
2 large basil leaves – chopped	0 calories
1 tablespoon lemon juice	4 calories
¼ teaspoon red pepper flakes	1 calorie
Dash of salt	0 calories

Method:

1. Chop it all up, toss it in a bowl and mix.
2. What could be easier?
3. Delicious!

DINNER
Around 200 Calories

Warm Asian Style Beef Salad

This hearty salad is the perfect way to end off your day. Succulent slices of sirloin steak pan-seared, tossed with salad greens and covered in a tangy dressing. The addition of sliced mango adds a sweetness to the flavor that is almost impossible to resist!

Prep Time : 10 minutes
Cook Time : 10 – 15 minutes (depending on how you like your steak)

Calories : **237**

Ingredients:

58g sirloin steak, lean only	139 calories
50g mango – cut into strips	35 calories
60g salad greens	16 calories
¼ red onion (28g) – sliced thinly	12 calories
1 teaspoon lime zest	1 calorie
1 teaspoon soy sauce	3 calories
½ teaspoon grated ginger	3 calories
½ teaspoon olive oil	20 calories
½ teaspoon sesame seeds – toasted	9 calories
Juice of ½ a lime (or about 1 tablespoon lime juice)	4 calories

Method:

1. Heat the olive oil in a non-stick pan over a medium high heat and cook the steak for about 5 minutes each side for medium-rare.
2. Remove the steak from the pan and allow to rest for 5 minutes and then slice into strips.
3. Meanwhile, toss the salad greens with the onions and mango and set aside.
4. In a small bowl, whisk the lime juice, lime zest, soy sauce and ginger together and pour it over the bowl of salad greens, tossing gently to combine.
5. Add the steak strips and finish off with a sprinkle of toasted sesame seeds.

Creamy Chicken and Rice Soup

This is a hearty, more filling version of classic cream of chicken soup. Adding some brown rice and potato bulks up the meal without raising the calorie count too much. Whip this up about half an hour, then sit back, relax and sip on your belly warming soup.

Prep Time	:	15 minutes
Cook Time	:	20 minutes
Calories	:	**247**

Ingredients:

250ml chicken stock	10 calories
30ml milk – 2% fat (or less)	15 calories
60g chicken breast – cut into cubes	99 calories
50g diced carrots	20 calories
50g diced potato	39 calories
1 tablespoon finely diced celery	1 calorie
1 tablespoon finely diced onion	4 calories
1 tablespoon brown rice	43 calories
½ teaspoon minced garlic	2 calories
½ teaspoon freshly chopped thyme	1 calorie
¼ teaspoon red pepper flakes	1 calorie
Non-stick cooking spray – 2 seconds	14 calories

Method:

1. Spray the bottom of a pot with a little cooking spray, then heat it up over a medium heat.
2. Sauté the onions, garlic and chicken cubes until they begin to turn brown and the chicken is cooked through.
3. Add the rest of the ingredients to the pot, turn up the heat and bring the pot to the boil.
4. Reduce the heat, cover and simmer for 15 minutes or until the veggies are soft. Serve hot – Enjoy!

Island Style Coriander Rice and Shrimp

Island Style Coriander Rice and Shrimp

This rice is so good that it has been elevated from a side dish to main meal status! Fluffy white rice combined with all your traditional Island flavors and spiced up with just a touch of red chili to turn up the heat dial. This is one meal you will make over and over.

Prep Time : 15 minutes
Cook Time : 15 minutes

Calories : **235**

Ingredients:

130g long grain white rice – cooked	169 calories
70g pineapple – chopped up small bite size pieces	35 calories
3 medium shrimp (19g) - peeled and deveined	20 calories
15g finely chopped coriander	3 calories
10g red chilli – seeds removed and finely diced	6 calories
½ tablespoon lime juice	2 calories

Method:

1. Cook the rice, drain, and place into a bowl.
2. While the rice is cooking, cook your shrimp by either boiling or grilling (depending on your preference.)
3. Add the shrimp and the rest of the ingredients to the bowl and toss well to combine.
4. Best served immediately.
5. Unbelievable!

*Note – you can swop the pineapple for other Island fruits for a varied taste every time. Both mango and pawpaw work very well, or you could add some shredded coconut or even a few pine nuts for something unique and different. Whatever you decide, you are guaranteed to fall in love with this dish. Don't forget to watch the calories!

Flavorful Chickpea Curry

Flavorful Chickpea Curry

This flavorful dish is wonderfully aromatic with strong Middle Eastern influences. Very filling and so quick and easy to prepare that you won't even miss the meat! But don't take my word for it – give it a try!

Prep Time	:	10 minutes
Cook Time	:	30 minutes
Calories	:	**235**

Ingredients:

60g chopped tomatoes	11 calories
50g chickpeas – drained	182 calories
¼ onion (28g) – chopped	12 calories
½ teaspoon olive oil	20 calories
½ teaspoon cumin	4 calories
½ teaspoon paprika	3 calories
¼ teaspoon grated ginger	2 calories
¼ teaspoon minced garlic	1 calorie
¼ teaspoon masala	0 calories

Method:

1. Heat up the olive oil in a non-stick pan over a medium heat and sauté the onions and garlic until the onions begin to soften.
2. Stir in the spices and cook for a further 5 minutes adding a little water if the pan gets too dry.
3. Now add the chickpeas, cover and cook for a further 5 minutes.
4. Lastly stir in the chopped tomatoes, cover and cook, stirring frequently.
5. Allow the curry to simmer for at least 10 minutes, but remember the longer you leave it the more the flavors develop.
6. Serve immediately and enjoy – this meal is out of this world!

Perfectly Posh Personal Pizza

Perfectly Posh Personal Pizza

Yes folks, you can even have pizza if you know how to cheat! This recipe uses a small tortilla as a pizza base, topped with succulent juicy steak and blue cheese. You will be hard pressed to remember what it is you like about regular pizza!

Prep Time	:	15 minutes
Cook Time	:	20 minutes
Calories	:	**238**

Ingredients:

1 corn tortilla (approx 6" diameter or 26 g)	58 calories
42g sirloin steak, lean only	101 calories
25g onion – sliced	11 calories
25g mushrooms – sliced	5 calories
1 tbsp blue cheese – crumbled	30 calories
1 tsp low fat mayonnaise	17 calories
1 tsp horseradish	2 calories
Non-stick cooking spray – 2 seconds	14 calories

Method:

1. Spray a non-stick pan with some cooking spray and heat it up over a medium heat.
2. Sauté the onions and mushrooms for about 5 minutes, or until they are beginning to soften, then remove them from the pan and set aside.
3. Add the steak to the pan and cook to your preferred level of doneness.
4. Allow the steak to rest for 5 minutes before slicing it paper thin.
5. Meanwhile, pop the tortilla into the oven at 200° C for about 3 – 5 minutes to crisp up a bit.
6. Mix the horseradish and mayonnaise together and spread it over the tortilla base, then top with the onion and mushroom mixture.
7. Add the steak slices and lastly add the crumbled blue cheese.
8. Return the pizza to the oven and bake for a further 5 minutes or until the cheese melts.
9. Slice, serve and be very woeful that you cannot have 2!

Quinoa and Sundried Tomatoes

Quinoa and Sundried Tomatoes

This dish is the quintessential skinny skillet supper. It's low in calories, tasty, filling and super easy to prepare. Who says diet food has to be bland and boring?

Prep Time   :   5 minutes
Cook Time   :   20 minutes

Calories   :   **243**

Ingredients:

43g quinoa, uncooked	158 calories
20g sundried tomatoes – diced	52 calories
125ml vegetable stock	10 calories
½ teaspoon olive oil	20 calories
¼ teaspoon minced garlic	1 calorie
¼ teaspoon oregano	1 calorie
¼ teaspoon red pepper flakes	1 calorie

Method:

1. Add the quinoa to a large saucepan and pour over the stock.
2. Cover and bring it to the boil, then reduce the heat and simmer for 15 minutes or until all the liquid has been absorbed.
3. In another pan, heat the olive oil over a medium heat, add the garlic and sundried tomatoes and sauté for 2 minutes.
4. Add the oregano and red pepper flakes and stir for another minute or two.
5. When the quinoa has absorbed all the liquid, stir in the sundried tomato mixture, cover and allow it to rest for 5 minutes before serving.
6. Tuck in! YUM!

Sage Pork Tenderloin with Apple and Sweet Potato Hash

Pan seared pork tenderloin medallions with a garlic and sage rub cooked to perfection and served with a classic apple and sweet potato hash – now that's good old fashioned comfort food at its best!

Prep Time : 10 minutes
Cook Time : 20 minutes

Calories : 247

Ingredients:

75g pork tenderloin, boneless & lean only	145 calories
60g apple – cored, peeled and cut into cubes	31 calories
60g sweet potato – peeled and cut into cubes	54 calories
1 teaspoon dried sage	2 calories
½ teaspoon garlic powder	5 calories
½ teaspoon cinnamon	3 calories
Non-stick cooking spray (1 second)	7 calories

Method:

1. Place the apples and sweet potatoes into a non-stick pan with a little water and cook, covered, over a medium heat until they are soft.
2. When they are tender, remove the lid, sprinkle on the cinnamon and turn up the heat to brown the mixture. Make sure you stir it often so it doesn't stick.
3. While this cooks, turn the broiler on high and allow it to heat up for at least 10 minutes.
4. Mix the sage and garlic powder together and rub it into the pork.
5. Place the pork into a broiling pan and cook until it is brown on one side (check after about 8 minutes). Once nicely browned flip and cook the other side.
6. Serve the pork with the apple hash on the side. Absolutely divine!

Pan Seared Scallops with Pea and Citrus Couscous

Pan-seared scallops cooked to perfection and accompanied by a savory pea couscous with subtle hints of citrus = totally delectable! This dish is amazing – you have been warned!

Prep Time	:	5 minutes
Cook Time	:	15 minutes
Calories	:	236

Ingredients:

85g scallops	95 calories
40g mange tout – halved	17 calories
26g couscous (uncooked)	94 calories
1 teaspoon orange zest	2 calories
1 teaspoon Italian seasoning	0 calories
Dash of pepper	0 calories
Salt to taste	0 calories
Non-stick cooking spray (4 seconds)	28 calories

Method:

1. Cook the couscous according to the package directions and set aside.
2. Spray some non-stick cooking spray (for 2 seconds) in a non-stick pan over a medium high heat. Add the scallops and cook until they are opaque throughout and turning golden (about 2 minutes on each side). Set aside.
3. Spray some non-stick cooking spray (2 seconds) into a non-stick pan and add the mange tout, about 1 tablespoon of water, and the orange zest.
4. Cook until the mange tout are just beginning to soften then add the couscous to the pan and mix it all together. Add your Italian seasoning.
5. Serve the scallops with the savory couscous dish on the side. So Tasty!

BREAKFAST
Under 300 Calories

French Toast with a Fruity Twist

Surprise center French toast – now that's a breakfast worth talking about! Crispy delicious golden French toast stuffed full of fresh blueberries makes this one meal that's definitely not to be missed! Very addictive – consider yourself warned!

Prep Time	:	15 minutes
Cook Time	:	15 minutes
Calories	:	**278**

Ingredients:

1 thick slice of French or Sourdough bread (1 3/4" thick)	185 calories
1 egg white	16 calories
48g blueberries	27 calories
2 teaspoons raw honey	43 calories
Non-stick cooking spray (1 second)	7 calories

Method:

1. Place the blueberries into a bowl and pour over the honey, taking care to ensure all the fruit is well coated
2. Very carefully cut a pocket horizontally into the slice of bread using a sharp knife.
3. Gently stuff the honey coated blueberries into the pocket, taking care not to break through the bread.
4. Whisk the egg white in a shallow dish and dip the stuffed bread into it, making sure both sides of the bread are coated in egg.
5. Now spray a non-stick pan with a little cooking spray and heat it up over a medium heat.
6. Cook the bread until golden brown on both sides, taking care when you turn the toast over that the berries don't fall out.
7. Serve immediately!

Egg, Kale, and Bacon Breakfast Bonanza

Egg, Kale, and Bacon Breakfast Bonanza

Drippy egg yolks oozing all over garlicky kale and crispy bacon as you cut open your perfectly toasted bun – a great start to any day! Slice, ooze, yum, repeat!

Prep Time	:	10 minutes
Cook Time	:	15 minutes
Calories	:	295

Ingredients:

1 hamburger bun (whole wheat is best) – toasted	120 calories
54g kale – thinly sliced	27 calories
1 slice extra lean turkey bacon (16g)	21 calories
1 large egg (50g)	72 calories
¼ teaspoon minced garlic	1 calorie
¼ teaspoon paprika	2 calories
½ tablespoon mayonnaise (optional)	45 calories
Non-stick cooking spray – 1 second	7 calories

Method:

1. Cook the bacon in a non-stick pan over a medium heat until very crispy.
2. Set the bacon aside on some paper towel and reserve the bacon drippings
3. Add the garlic and kale to the pan that you cooked the bacon in and cook over a medium high heat until the kale is tender.
4. Slice the bun in half and place the kale onto the bottom half of the bun and top with the bacon.
5. Spray the non-stick cooking spray and cook your egg until the white is set but the yolk is still soft.
6. Place the egg onto the bacon and sprinkle it with a little paprika then top with the other half of the bun.
7. Slice the bun in half, see the yolk pool on the plate and gobble it up!
8. I won't even judge you if you don't make it to the dining room table to eat!

*Note – If you have any leftover kale crisps/chips (for which you can find the recipe in my previous 5:2 diet book), then they work even *better* with this recipe!

Single Girl Cinnamon Vanilla Drop Scones

Single Girl Cinnamon Vanilla Drop Scones

Sometimes you have just got to have something sweet to start your day. When those days strike, here is the perfect recipe, with just the right quantity to make 2 large sized drop scones, while still keeping your calories in check. This one is best served with some unsweetened applesauce as a low calorie syrup alternative (just be sure to add 7 calories for every tablespoon of applesauce).

Prep Time	:	10 minutes
Cook Time	:	10 minutes
Calories	:	**300**

Ingredients:

42g wholemeal flour	153 calories
60ml unsweetened vanilla almond milk	10 calories
1 large egg (50g)	72 calories
1 teaspoon vegetable oil	40 calories
½ teaspoon cinnamon	3 calories
½ teaspoon vanilla	6 calories
½ teaspoon baking powder	2 calories
¼ teaspoon baking soda	0 calories
Dash of salt	0 calories
Non-stick cooking spray – 2 seconds	14 calories

Method:

1. Mix all the dry ingredients together in a bowl.
2. Whisk all the wet ingredients except for the applesauce together in a bowl.
3. Whisk the dry ingredients into the wet ingredients until they are just combined – do not over mix.
4. Spray a non-stick pan (or griddle) with some cooking spray (for 1 second) and heat it up over a medium high heat.
5. Pour 1/2 of the batter into the pan and let it cook until the surface starts to bubble, then flip it over and cook the other side.
6. Repeat with the rest of the batter.
7. Serve with some warmed applesauce.
8. Absolute sinful indulgence – enjoy!

Spanish Coffee Cup Scramble

This healthy egg breakfast literally takes minutes to prepare. The perfect meal for those mornings when you over sleep – just throw the ingredients into your coffee mug, zap it in the microwave and voila – BREAKFAST!

Prep Time	:	Under 5 minutes
Cook Time	:	Under 5 minutes
Calories	:	**291**

Ingredients:

72g frozen shredded hash browns	191 calories
1 small egg (38g)	55 calories
1 tablespoon corn and black bean salsa	10 calories
1 tablespoon water	0 calories
1 tablespoon cheddar cheese – shredded	28 calories
Dash of salt and pepper	0 calories
Non-stick cooking spray – 1 second	7 calories

Method:

1. Spray a large microwaveable coffee mug (about 12 ounces) with some cooking spray.
2. Place the frozen hash browns into the mug and microwave on high for 1 minute.
3. Whisk the egg together with the water. Season the egg mixture with salt and pepper and pour the mixture into the coffee cup.
4. Put the cup back into the microwave for 30 seconds, then stir and microwave for another 30 seconds.
5. Keep doing this until the eggs are cooked to your taste.
6. Remove the mug from the microwave and sprinkle over the cheese while the egg is hot so it melts.
7. Top with the salsa and serve.
8. Quick, easy, and totally divine!

Cheesy Grits and Greens

This good old fashioned Southern dish provides a comforting breakfast on those lazy mornings when you just want to languish in bed for those extra few minutes (all the better if you can get someone to serve it to you in bed!).

Prep Time	:	15 minutes
Cook Time	:	30 minutes
Calories	:	**279**

Ingredients:

80ml vegetable broth	13 calories
112g kale – roughly chopped	55 calories
40g yellow grits (uncooked)	148 calories
14g sharp cheddar cheese – shredded or grated	57 calories
1 garlic clove – minced	4 calories
1 tsp lemon juice	1 calorie
1/8 teaspoon red pepper flakes	1 calorie
Dash of salt and pepper	0 calories

Method:

1. Place the vegetable stock along with 160ml of water into a pot and bring it to a boil.
2. Add the grits to the water and cook for 20 minutes, stirring often.
3. While the grits cook, rinse your kale and bring a big pot of cold water to a boil. Add a 1/2 tsp of salt to the water.
4. Submerge the chopped kale into the water and cook for about 5 minutes or until kale is a little chewy but not tough.
5. Drain kale, set it aside, and add 1 tsp of lemon juice over the kale.
6. When the grits are cooked, stir in half the cheese, garlic, and red pepper flakes. Season with some salt and pepper.
7. Place the grits on a plate and top with the remaining cheese and lemon kale.
8. Unbelievable taste – enjoy!

Baked Avocado Boats

Baked Avocado Boats

Simple, elegant and unusual, these avocado boats are a dream! They are so easy to make and taste so good that you will have to exert extraordinary self-control to stop at just one.

Prep Time	:	Under 5 minutes
Cook Time	:	20 minutes
Calories	:	**285**

Ingredients:

an avocado half (100g) – pit removed but skin still on	160 calories
1 medium egg (44g)	70 calories
½ teaspoon garlic powder	5 calories
¼ teaspoon paprika	2 calories
1/2 teaspoon of lime juice	1 calorie
1 slice of Canadian bacon/back bacon (29g)	44 calories
½ tablespoon of pico de gallo or 1 cherry tomato chopped	3 calories

Method:

1. Cook the slice of Canadian bacon until crispy. Chop finely and set aside.
2. Scrape out just enough of the avocado to accommodate an egg and sprinkle the avocado with lime juice and garlic powder.
3. Carefully crack an egg into the hollow taking care to keep the yolk intact.
4. Sprinkle the paprika over the top.
5. Place the boat onto a baking tray and bake at 180° C for about 15 minutes or until the white of the egg is set.
6. Remove from the oven and allow to cool slightly.
7. Top with the bacon crumbles and pico de gallo.
8. Grab a spoon and tuck in. YUM!

*Note – If you prefer, substitute the slice of Canadian bacon for a slice of toasted whole wheat multi grain bread instead and spoon out the avocado, egg, and pico de gallo mixture on the toast! INCREDIBLE and only a total of 286 calories!

Tex-Mex Scramble

Bits of tortilla, salsa and cheese all scrambled up with some eggs, onions and jalapenos – DROOL! This breakfast is so easy to make and packs a major flavor punch. A great way to start your day!

Prep Time	:	10 minutes
Cook Time	:	15 minutes
Calories	:	**297**

Ingredients:

2 small eggs (38g each) – beaten	126 calories
1 corn tortilla (24g) – cut up into strips	58 calories
2 tablespoons cheddar cheese – grated	57 calories
2 tablespoons salsa	9 calories
1 tablespoons onion – diced	5 calories
1 tablespoon jalapeno pepper – chopped	2 calories
1 teaspoon olive oil	40 calories

Method:

1. Heat the olive oil in a non-stick pan over a medium heat and add the tortilla pieces.
2. Cook until they start to turn brown, then add the jalapenos and onions to the pan and sauté until they begin to soften.
3. Add the salsa and stir constantly while it cooks for about a minute, then pour in the eggs.
4. Cook the eggs to your desired consistency, stirring often.
5. When the eggs are done to your liking, sprinkle over the cheese and keep the pan over the heat until the cheese melts.
6. Serve immediately!
7. Absolutely to die for!

LUNCH
Under 300 Calories

Toasted Apple Bacon 'n Cheddar Panini

Toasted Apple Bacon 'n Cheddar Panini

These amazing pan-fried sandwiches are gooey deliciousness at its finest. Golden brown and crispy on the outside, contrasted with the tartness of the apples and the soft melted cheese and honey mustard, this is a taste sensation not to be missed!

Prep Time	:	10 minutes
Cook Time	:	10 minutes
Calories	:	**299**

Ingredients:

2 slices light multi-grain bread	90 calories
½ granny smith apple (75g) – sliced paper thin	39 calories
1 slice of cheddar cheese (28g)	113 calories
1 slice extra lean turkey bacon (15g), cooked crisp	30 calories
2 teaspoons honey mustard	20 calories
Non-stick cooking spray – 1 second	7 calories

Method:

1. Spray a non-stick pan with a light layer of cooking spray (for 1 second).
2. Spread each slice of bread with 1 teaspoon of honey mustard.
3. Place the apple slices on one slice of bread and top with the slice of cheddar cheese and bacon. Place the last slice of bread on top.
4. Heat the prepared pan over a medium heat on the stove.
5. When it's hot, add the sandwich and cook until brown on both sides and cheese is melted.
6. Remove from the pan, slice and serve.
7. Scrumptious!

*Note – You can find a good light multi-grain bread 45 calories per slice (or less), readily available in most supermarkets. Also, you can reduce the calorie intake of this recipe by choosing a slice of low fat cheddar cheese at just 50 calories, bringing you total to just 213 calories!

Crumbed Cod Burgers

These crumbed cod burgers are simplicity personified! Forget Mickey D's because these will blow you away. Completely fool proof, totally delicious and under 300 calories. It's a no-brainer folks!

Prep Time	:	10 minutes
Cook Time	:	15 minutes
Calories	:	**299**

Ingredients:

1 whole wheat hamburger bun – split and toasted	120 calories
100g cod fillet (Atlantic tastes best)	80 calories
1 romaine lettuce leaf	1 calorie
10g onion (1 slice)	4 calories
10g tomato (1 slice)	2 calories
2 tablespoons dry bread crumbs	53 calories
1 tablespoon fat-free yogurt	6 calories
1 tablespoon fat-free mayonnaise	29 calories
½ teaspoon lemon juice	1 calorie
1 pinch onion flakes	1 calorie
1 pinch garlic powder	1 calorie
1 pinch cayenne pepper	1 calorie
1 pinch dried parsley	0 calories
1 pinch lemon zest	0 calories

Method:

1. Mix the bread crumbs with the garlic powder, cayenne pepper, lemon zest and dried parsley.
2. Coat the cod fillet with the bread crumb mixture and place it onto a baking tray under the broiler for 5 minutes on each side or until the fish flakes easily with a fork.
3. While the fish cooks, mix the mayonnaise, yogurt, lemon juice and onion flakes together and spread the mixture over the cut sides of the hamburger bun.
4. Top one half of the hamburger bun with the lettuce, tomato and onion.
5. When the fish is cooked, place it on top of the salad and top with the second half of the bun.
6. Eat immediately and revel in sheer delight at the flavor!

Mint Cucumber Yogurt Bowl

Mint Cucumber Yogurt Bowl

The classic combination of dill, feta cheese, cucumber, and yogurt has become somewhat of diet royalty – not least of all because it is absolutely delicious! This recipe takes that classic combo and dials it up a notch by adding some minced garlic and mint for a load of more flavor.

Prep Time	:	20 minutes
Cook Time	:	0 minutes
Calories	:	**274**

Ingredients:

2 cucumbers (602g total) – peeled and chopped into bite size pieces	94 calories
65g non-fat Greek yogurt	39 calories
42g feta cheese – crumbled	111 calories
6g fresh dill weed – finely chopped	17 calories
2 garlic cloves, minced	10 calories
Several sprigs fresh mint, finely chopped	2 calories
¼ tsp black pepper	1 calorie
Salt to taste	0 calories

Method:

1. Place the cucumbers and the dill in a bowl.
2. Add the yogurt and stir to make sure the salad is well coated.
3. Gently fold in the feta cheese, taking care not to over mix.
4. Season with some salt and black pepper and serve straight away.
5. A healthy scrumptious lunch does not get easier than this!

*Note – This recipe tastes even better refrigerated overnight. Enjoy!

Fab Pecan Egg Salad

This is a taste sensation second to none. Egg salad has never been jazzed up like this before – crunchy apples provide just the right amount of sweetness to offset the tartness of the onions and throwing in a few pecans adds a delicious textured crunch. Your favorite curry powder blend completes this meal perfectly by adding a mild spicy undertone to an otherwise plain salad. Mix it all up with a little plain yogurt instead of the traditional mayonnaise and you have yourself an incredibly tasty low calorie salad that will leave you salivating!

Prep Time	:	Time to boil eggs + 5 minutes
Cook Time	:	0 minutes
Calories	:	**297**

Ingredients:

2 large boiled eggs	156 calories
28g onion – finely chopped	12 calories
¼ apple (40g) – chopped	21 calories
56g non-fat plain Greek yogurt	35 calories
1 tablespoon pecans – toasted and roughly chopped	65 calories
1 teaspoon curry powder (your favorite)	7 calories
Bunch chives – minced	1 calorie
Pinch salt	0 calories

Method:

1. Peel the boiled eggs and place them in a bowl.
2. Mash the eggs up with a fork. Don't overdo it as it is nice to have a bit of texture in the final product.
3. Add the onions, apples and chives and mix together well.
4. Now mix the curry powder and yogurt together in a bowl and pour it over the salad, taking care to mix and ensure it is evenly distributed through the other ingredients.
5. Lastly add the pecans, season with some salt and give it one last stir.
6. Serve immediately.

Kiwi Coconut Shrimp and Greens

This is the perfect meal for those days when you just feel really indulgent and what better way to celebrate indulgence than with seafood. The unusual pairing of shrimp with kiwi fruit is not only unique but tremendously tasty especially when combined with the subtle citrus flavors in the dressing and coconut. This is a NICE size serving. Hope you're hungry.

Prep Time	:	10 minutes
Cook Time	:	10 minutes
Calories	:	**290**

Ingredients:

7 medium shrimp (46g) – peeled and deveined	49 calories
180g baby spinach leaves	50 calories
1 kiwi fruit (70g) – chopped	43 calories
20g desiccated coconut	71 calories
1 tablespoon rice vinegar	10 calories
1 tablespoon spring onions – chopped	2 calories
1 tablespoon chopped coriander	0 calories
1 tablespoon lemon juice	4 calories
½ tablespoon olive oil	60 calories
1 teaspoon lemon zest	1 calorie

Method:

1. Cook your shrimp by either boiling or grilling them (depending on your preference).
2. Place the baby spinach leaves in a salad bowl and top with the kiwi fruit and the shrimp
3. Combine the rest of the ingredients (except for the desiccated coconut) in a small bowl and mix. Pour the dressing over the salad and toss well to mix.
4. Top the salad with the shredded coconut.
5. Tuck in! YUM!

Ham & Chilies Pizza Muffins

Ham & Chilies Pizza Muffins

These little "pizzas" are the perfect lunch time meal. Quick, low calorie and 100% versatile, you just cannot go wrong. Change the toppings to suit your mood and create a different culinary masterpiece every single time. This recipe makes 2 pizza muffins.

Prep Time	:	10 minutes
Cook Time	:	10 minutes
Calories	:	**293**

Ingredients:

1 Whole Wheat or Multi-Grain English muffin – cut in half horizontally	Up to 130 calories
30g ham – chopped	49 calories
21g mozzarella cheese	63 calories
25g onion – diced	11 calories
10g chopped green chilies	32 calories
2 medium fresh tomato slices (1/4" thick or 20g each)	8 calories

Method:

1. Preheat oven to 230°C.
2. Place the muffin halves cut side up onto a baking tray.
3. Arrange the toppings evenly on both halves, making sure the mozzarella cheese is placed on the bottom, the tomato on top of the cheese, and the onions, ham, and green chilies, placed on top.
4. Pop the baking tray under the broiler for about 6-8 minutes or until the toppings are nicely browned, but not burnt.
5. Eat up! This is gooey deliciousness at its best – enjoy!

*Note – Be sure to double check the calorie count for the English muffin. Some brands (like Thomas English whole wheat muffins) are 120 calories rather than 130 calories, which would save you 10 calories.

Spicy Veggie Chowder

Spicy Veggie Chowder

This creamy soup is crammed full of nutritious veggie goodness that will keep you full until supper time without being too heavy on the tummy. A touch of chili and cayenne spice up an otherwise ordinary dish with enough flavor to rev your metabolism into fat-burning gear!

Prep Time	:	20 minutes
Cook Time	:	30 minutes
Calories	:	**299**

Ingredients:

250ml vegetable stock	15 calories
70g potatoes – peeled and cubed	52 calories
75g carrots – peeled and chopped	28 calories
75g creamed corn	54 calories
1 low fat mozzarella cheese stick, cut into cube-like pieces	85 calories
40g mushrooms – sliced	9 calories
60ml milk (2% fat or less)	31 calories
25g onion – chopped	11 calories
25g red pepper – chopped	8 calories
¼ teaspoon minced garlic	1 calorie
¼ teaspoon cayenne pepper – or to taste	1 calorie
1 red chili (10g) – seeds removed and finely chopped	4 calories

Method:

1. Place the potatoes, carrots, onions, garlic, chili and red pepper into a saucepan and cover with the vegetable stock.
2. Bring the pot to the boil, then reduce the heat and simmer for 15 minutes or until the vegetables are tender.
3. Add the corn, milk, mushrooms and cayenne pepper to the pot and stir well. Cook for a further 5 minutes or until heated through.
4. Just before you are ready to serve, turn off the heat and stir in the cheddar cheese. Keep the pot over the heat until the cheese has melted, then transfer to your serving bowl.
5. Sip slowly and enjoy! Sublimely superb!

DINNER
Under 300 Calories

Garlic Tilapia with Sundried Tomato Couscous

This simple meal embodies elegance with every mouthful. Small amounts of powerful ingredients revs this dish up from bland to excellent and achieves this all in about 30 minutes. Not much more you can ask from a low-calorie dinner.

Prep Time	:	10 minutes + 10 minutes marinating time
Cook Time	:	10 minutes
Calories	:	298

Ingredients:

87g tilapia fillet	112 calories
35g couscous (uncooked)	132 calories
5 sundried tomatoes – chopped	25 calories
1 tablespoon freshly chopped parsley	1 calorie
1 tablespoon lemon juice	4 calories
1 teaspoon crushed garlic	4 calories
½ teaspoon olive oil	20 calories

Method:

1. Mix the lemon juice, garlic and oil together and coat the tilapia with the mixture.
2. Allow it to marinade for 10 minutes to really absorb the flavors.
3. Cook the couscous as per the package directions.
4. When it is cooked, stir it in a bowl with the sundried tomatoes and parsley.
5. Now heat up the grill and place the tilapia onto the grill for about 2 minutes per side or until cooked through. (You can also choose to bake it).
6. Serve with the savory couscous and enjoy.
7. What a meal!

Spicy Shrimp Linguine

Spicy Shrimp Linguine

Shrimp and pasta in a creamy sauce – YUM! This is a quick and simple dish that is totally delicious. Spice up the dish with a dash of chili powder or Cajun seasoning if you are feeling adventurous or simply serve it as is for those who have a more sensitive palate. Either way – it's amazing!

Prep Time	:	10 minutes
Cook Time	:	25 minutes
Calories	:	**296**

Ingredients:

7 medium sized shrimp (46g)– peeled and deveined	49 calories
125ml chicken stock	5 calories
60ml water	0 calories
40ml milk - 2% fat (or less)	21 calories
50g linguine pasta, uncooked	179 calories
40g mushrooms – sliced	9 calories
20g red bell pepper – chopped	6 calories
1 tablespoon freshly chopped parsley	1 calorie
Non-stick cooking spray (3 seconds)	21 calories
½ teaspoon flour	5 calories

Method:

1. Place the chicken stock and water into a Dutch oven and bring it to a boil. Then add the pasta and simmer for about 10 minutes.
2. Add the shrimp to the pan and cook until they are done (about 3 – 5 minutes).
3. Drain the shrimp and pasta and set aside.
4. Spray a non-stick pan some non-stick cooking spray (for 3 seconds) over a medium heat. Add the mushrooms and red pepper and sauté until they begin to soften (about 5 minutes), stirring frequently.
5. Add the flour to the pan and then the milk and stir constantly until the sauce thickens.
6. Pour the sauce over the shrimp and pasta, sprinkle with parsley and serve.

Mexican Stuffed Potatoes

There is nothing more comforting than a baked potato! And when it is combined with chicken and some Mexicana style toppings the humble baked potato gets elevated to new heights. This dish is crammed full of some of the best flavors and promises to become a firm household favorite!

Prep Time	:	10 minutes
Cook Time	:	25 minutes
Calories	:	**297**

Ingredients:

1 small potato (170g)	131 calories
40g chicken breast – cooked and cubed	66 calories
1 tablespoon cheddar cheese – shredded	28 calories
20g chili beans	22 calories
20g spring onions – sliced	6 calories
1 tablespoon barbeque sauce	23 calories
1 tablespoon fat free sour cream	9 calories
½ teaspoon garlic salt	5 calories
½ teaspoon chopped parsley	0 calorie
Non-stick cooking spray – 1 second	7 calories

Method:

1. Pierce the potato with a fork after washing it well and removing any blemishes.
2. Spray the potato with some cooking spray (for 1 second) and rub the outside of it with the garlic salt and parsley.
3. Place it onto a microwave safe plate and cook on high for about 5 minutes. Keep checking the potato as you don't want to overcook it – it should be tender, but still firm.
4. Slice the potato in half and scoop out some of the flesh, leaving a ½ centimeter shell around the edge.
5. Place the scooped out potato into a bowl and mix it with the cooked chicken and barbeque sauce.
6. Now spoon the mixture back into the potato shells.
7. Top with the beans, spring onions and lastly the cheese.
8. Place on a baking tray and put it into the oven for 15 minutes on 180° C or until the cheese has melted and is bubbly and brown.
9. Serve immediately with a tablespoon of fat free sour cream. Scrumptious!

Pepperoni Pizza Pasta

Pepperoni Pizza Pasta

Pepperoni – good! Pizza – good! Pasta – good! All three together – OUT OF THIS WORLD! This is one of those meals that remind you that dieting does not equate to carrot sticks and can be fun and enjoyable! Guaranteed to become a firm favorite on those days when you're craving pasta.

Prep Time	:	5 minutes
Cook Time	:	15 minutes
Calories	:	**291**

Ingredients:

140g whole wheat pasta (preferably bow-tie or similar), cooked	174 calories
60ml tomato purée	15 calories
6 pepperoni slices (12g) – quartered	60 calories
14g fresh mozzarella – chopped	42 calories
1 teaspoon Italian seasoning	0 calories

Method:

1. Place the cooked pasta, tomato purée, half the pepperoni and Italian seasoning into an oven proof bowl and mix.
2. Add the rest of the pepperoni and mozzarella on top and place it under the broiler until the cheese has melted and the pasta is warmed through (about 5 minutes).
3. Serve immediately and enjoy.
4. Absolutely scrumptious!

*Note – Looking for another pasta alternative lower in calories? Replace the whole wheat pasta with spaghetti squash! It takes a little longer to prepare, but it is so SO worth it. Did I mention that 1 cup or 140g of cooked spaghetti squash is only 43 calories! Replace the whole wheat pasta with spaghetti squash for a much lower total of 164 calories. Lastly, if you have no fresh mozzarella on hand, you can use a tbsp. of grated parmesan cheese instead at just 20 calories per tbsp.

Sweet Potato and Spinach Quesadilla

Tortillas baked to crispy golden perfection and stuffed full of sweet potato mash, black beans, spinach, and gooey stringy mozzarella cheese – dinner has never been better! This is so good you won't even feel like you are on a diet!

Prep Time	:	15 minutes
Cook Time	:	15 minutes
Calories	:	**295**

Ingredients:

30g baby spinach	7 calories
1 sweet potato (130g) – skin removed	99 calories
50g tinned black beans – drained	40 calories
20g part skim mozzarella cheese – shredded	51 calories
1 medium (approx 6" dia) (30g) flour tortilla	90 calories
1 tablespoon red onion – chopped	4 calories
½ tablespoon lime juice	2 calories
¼ tsp cumin or chili powder	2 calories

Method:

1. Microwave the sweet potato on high until it is tender (about 10 minutes). Alternatively you can peel the sweet potato, chop into cubes, and boil until soft.
2. When the potato is cooked, sauté the onions in a non-stick pan over a medium heat until they begin to caramelize. (Add a bit of water if necessary).
3. Drain and rinse the black beans. Tinned beans are already cooked, so microwave them just enough to warm them up. Set aside.
4. Remove the sweet potato flesh and mash it very nicely in a bowl with some cumin or chili powder.
5. Spread out the tortilla, and on one half spread out the sweet potato mash, and top with the spinach, onions, beans, and cheese. Sprinkle with lime juice. Fold over the other half of the tortilla.
6. Bake the tortilla in the oven at 190°C for 8-10 minutes, or until the tortilla is brown and the cheese has melted.
7. Transfer the quesadilla to a plate, slice it in half and know you won't make it to the table before having a huge bite!

*Note – If you'd like to save more calories, eliminate the tortilla all together, and enjoy all of the cooked ingredients in a bowl! Sweet potatoes, spinach, and beans are incredibly scrumptious all by themselves.

Chili & Cinnamon Pork w/ Sweet Bourbon Sauce ¹²⁸

Chili and Cinnamon Pork with Sweet Bourbon Sauce

This is one of those splash out and treat yourself meals! The flavors marry together in the most exquisite way to produce a truly unbelievable dining experience.

Prep Time	:	10 minutes
Cook Time	:	15 minutes
Calories	:	**290**

Ingredients:

85g pork sirloin chop – boneless and lean only	164 calories
30ml bourbon	65 calories
1 tablespoon brown sugar	34 calories
2 tablespoons soy sauce	16 calories
1 tablespoon balsamic vinegar	3 calories
1 teaspoon crushed garlic	4 calories
¼ teaspoon chili powder	2 calories
¼ teaspoon cinnamon	1 calorie
Pinch allspice	1 calorie
Pinch of salt	0 calories

Method:

1. Combine the spices together and rub them into the pork well. Allow the pork to rest for 5 minutes to absorb the spices.
2. To make the sauce – combine the bourbon, garlic, soy sauce, balsamic, and brown sugar in a saucepan and bring the mixture to a boil. Allow it to cook for about 5 minutes, stirring occasionally. Set aside half of the sauce.
3. Preheat broiler.
4. Broil the pork about 4 inches from the heat for about 5 minutes on each side, basting occasionally with half the sauce. (Thermometer should read at least 145° when pork is cooked thoroughly).
5. Serve the pork with remaining sauce drizzled over it.

Super Easy Chili

There is nothing like a bowl of hot chili on a cold day...or a hot day....or any day really! This is an easy and classic recipe that will fill your belly and warm your soul. Just be sure to have a big glass of water handy!

Prep Time	:	Less than 5 minutes
Cook Time	:	20 minutes
Calories	:	**296**

Ingredients:

100g minced turkey – 85% lean, 15% fat	150 calories
100g tinned kidney beans, drained	85 calories
300g tinned Del Monte diced tomatoes	53 calories
1 tablespoon chopped onion	4 calories
½ teaspoon chili powder	4 calories

Method:

1. In a nonstick saucepan cook the onions, and turkey, stirring frequently, until the meat is cooked through.
2. Add the rest of the ingredients, stir to combine, bring to a boil, then lower heat to medium-low. Cover and cook for 15 minutes.
3. Serve hot!

CONCLUSION

And that's a wrap folks! If you are looking for a custom-made, personally tailored eating regime that fits seamlessly into your life, you have just hit the jackpot. This diet invites you to take responsibility for your health, weight and life and gives you the freedom to make healthy, sensible food choices every single day (while allowing you those much needed days of indulgence). And the absolute cherry on top is that you are not forced or expected to endure the endless hunger that is characteristic of most other reduced calorie diets.

If you cannot enjoy what you are eating, your days on a diet are numbered. The fast diet has longevity and can be followed long term with ease because it is more about creating healthier lifestyle changes. Its primary focus is on developing a balance in your life and a healthy relationship with food. So what are you waiting for? It's time to reap the benefits of good health and unveil a slimmer trimmer you! Enjoy.

Recommendations... Hungry for More?

Want *more* low calorie goodness? Be sure to purchase the original "5:2 Diet Recipe Book' by Diana Clayton. Between these two books combined, there's just no way you will *ever* run out of incredibly delicious and enticing low calorie meals for your fasting days. Bon Appétit!

Thank you for your purchase! If you enjoyed this book, please consider leaving a review at Amazon. Even if it's just a line or two, I read every one and it would make all the difference. :) Thank you!